IN DEFENCE OF
THE FOUR IMAMS

To Order Islamic Books
Kitab House, Inc.
www.KitabHouse.com
(404) 585 8177

IN DEFENCE OF
THE FOUR IMAMS
IBN TAYMIYAH

CLARITAS
BOOKS

For all lovers and seekers of truth.

1 2 3 4 5 6 7 8 9 10

CLARITAS BOOKS

Bernard Street, Swansea, United Kingdom
Milpitas, California, United States

© CLARITAS BOOKS 2018

This book is in copyright. Subject to statutory exception and to the provisions of relevant collective licensing agreements, no reproduction of any part may take place without the written permission of
Claritas Books.

First Published in January 2018

Typeset in Minion Pro 14/11
Printed by Mega Printing in Turkey

In Defence Of The Four Imams
by Ibn Taymiyah
Translated by Abdullah bin Hamid Ali

A CIP catalogue record for this book is available from the British Library

ISBN: 978-1-905837-63-2

Ibn Taymiyah was born in Harran in the year 661 AH, and his father and family relocated to Damascus in his youth. In Damascus he embarked upon his formal studies with a number of the major scholars of the city and excelled in hadith, fiqh, tafsir, and other sciences. He was known to be a major depository of knowledge until it was said of him that he had greater mastery of the various legal schools than even their exponents among his contemporaries. He was reverentially referred to as "Shaykh al-Islam" by those who respected him. And, the great Shafi'i contemporary Ibn al-Zamlakani reportedly said of him, "The conditions of juristic independence (*ijtihad*) were brought together in their appropriate fashion with respect to him." But, like so many others before him, Ibn Taymiyah was tested by both the limitations of his knowledge and the jealousy of some of his peers. Consequently, much of his life was spent imprisoned in the Damascus citadel due to being perceived as a threat to Islamic orthodoxy and public order. A number of scholars deemed him an ideological threat and succeeded in convincing the governors that his detention would best serve society. It would seem, judging by the massive numbers of those reported to have attended his funeral (an excess of between 65,000 to 200,000 persons), that the attempts to silence him and limit his influence failed. Among those greatly influenced by his views were his students: the Hanbali jurist Ibn Qayyim al-Jawziyah, the Shafi'i exegete Abu al-Fida' Ibn Kathir, the Shafi'i hadith master Al-Hafiz Al-Dhahabi, and the Hanafi theologian Ibn Abi al-'Izz. A number of scholars wrote in opposition to some of his views that broke with the Sunni orthodoxy at the time, some even accusing him of unbelief (*kufr*). Others acknowledged his virtue, knowledge, piety, and mastery of the sciences, including the Shafi'i renewer (*mujaddid*) Ibn Daqiq al-'Id. Several heterodoxic views have been attributed to Ibn Taymiyah, while a number of his defenders have denied them as smears launched against him by his enemies. His demise was met in the prison of the Damascus citadel in the year 728 AH and was buried in the "Cemetery of the Sufis" (*Maqbarah al-Sufiyah*) next to his brother, Sharaf al-Din 'Abd Allah.

Contents

TRANSLATOR'S INTRODUCTION	13
INTRODUCTION	21

THE FIRST CAUSE
He was unaware of the hadith ... 23

THE SECOND CAUSE
He was aware of the hadith, but it wasn't sound in his view ... 31

THE THIRD CAUSE
He believes the hadith presented by those differing with him is weak ... 33

THE FOURTH CAUSE
He Stipulates Conditions for the Reports of Reliable Narrators that are different from other scholars ... 37

THE FIFTH CAUSE
He knew the hadith, considered it to be genuine, but forgot it ... 39

THE SIXTH CAUSE
He did not know what the hadith meant ... 41

THE SEVENTH CAUSE
He believes that his opponent misconstrues the hadith ... 45

THE EIGHTH CAUSE
    He believes that the interpretation conflicts with something else that shows that the intent is other than what his opponent says   47

THE NINTH CAUSE
    He believes that the hadith is contravened by something that indicates that it is weak, or it is abrogated, or its meaning is figurative—if it is subject to being taken figuratively and reassigned a different meaning by something accepted as valid by consensus, like a Quranic verse, another hadith, or scholarly consensus   49

THE TENTH CAUSE
    He believes that the hadith opposes what proves that it is weak, abrogated, or reassigned a figurative meaning while other scholars do not share his view. Or the category of what is mentioned in the hadith is in opposition to something, or it is really not in opposition to anything. Rather, it is weightier.   53

APPENDIX   101
    CHAPTER 1   103
    CHAPTER 2   105
    CHAPTER 3   107
    CHAPTER 4   109

NOTES   123

BIOGRAPHY   163

Translator's Introduction

Shaykh al-Islam Ahmad b. Taymiyah - may Allah abound him with His mercy - was one of the most brilliant, though controversial, minds in Islamic history. Many Muslims in the circles of the learned and unlearned alike would like to write him out of the history books. But it would seem that Allah ﷻ has made it so that his name will be eternalised as one of the most prominent figures of Islamic history, on par with figures like The Four Imams, Abu Hamid al-Ghazali, mystics like Ibn 'Arabi and Rumi, philosophers like Ibn Sina (Avicenna) and Ibn Rushd (Averroes), and many others.

Ibn Taymiyah may not shine as bright as any of the Four Imams, but he has exuded a light brilliant enough not to go without notice. This does not mean that he is free of any error in his thought, reasoning, or approach. Rather, he - as with all others - was tested by the limits of his mental faculties and reason until he was plunged into very dangerous territory leaving him the subject of mainstream critiques. In some matters, he was accused of contravening unanimous consensus (*ijma'*). And in other matters, he is believed to have violated the sanctity of the pure and pristine Islamic doctrine as connoted by the Quran and the prophetic tradition in spite of his claim that he was following the approach of the Pious Forbearers, *The Salaf*.

In this book of his, *Raf' al-Malamm 'an al-I'immat al-'Alam* (Removing Blame from the Distinguished Imams), he offers a number of excuses that remove the accusation of sin from the Four Imams and others like them for not acting in accord with certain prophetic traditions (hadiths). This is especially important in this day and age because there are many who have accused some of the Imams of ruling in contravention to the Sunnah of Allah's messenger ﷺ due to not knowing or understanding their reasoning for not applying a particular hadith. It is also important because those who usually, implicitly or explicitly, launch such accusations are those who champion the views of Ibn Taymiyah in a number of matters, especially his doctrine concerning the divine attributes.

This championing of his views by such people has led to their opponents - who are ignorant of many of the works of the shaykh - to assume that Ibn Taymiyah was also one of those who exhibited intolerance with legal differences and that he was one who condemned anyone for following one of the four surviving Sunni schools of Islamic law (*fiqh*). On the contrary, Ibn Taymiyah was himself an adherent of the Hanbali School of law, and Ibn Al-Zamlakani[1] praised him as being one of those who reached the level of *mujtahid* in the school.[2]

Consequently, this book will serve to many as the clearest sign that much of what is attributed to Ibn Taymiyah or is thought of him is untrue in the same way that it is untrue that Ibn Taymiyah denied all forms of theoretical and practical Sufism. This is believed in spite of the fact that he dedicates a complete volume of his Collection of Fatwas (*Majmu' al-Fatawa*) to the topic of Sufism[3], which he and his student Ibn Qayim al-Jawziyah referred to many times as *'Ilm as-Suluk'* —Behavioural Science.

Ibn Taymiyah says in this book about the excuses given for the Imams,

"And [I] let it be known that there is not one of the Imams who is universally accepted by the Ummah who intentionally contradicts the Messenger of Allah ﷺ in any of his Sunnah whether small or large. For they surely agree with certainty upon the obligation of following the Messenger ﷺ and upon the fact that every person has statements that can be accepted and [others that] can be rejected contrary to [the case of] Allah's messenger ﷺ. However, when a statement of one of them is found that a sound hadith contradicts, there must be an excuse in their abandonment of it. And all [legitimate] excuses are of three classifications: *The first of them*: is his belief that the Prophet ﷺ did not say it. *The second*: is his belief that that particular issue was not intended by that statement. *And the third*: is his belief that that ruling is abrogated."

Then, he says, "And these three classifications branch out into a variety of causes." He, then, proceeds to list ten causes that lead them to their beliefs, which are:

1. He was unaware of the hadith.
2. He was aware of the hadith, but it was not sound in his view.
3. He believed the hadith presented by those differing with him to be weak.
4. He stipulates conditions for the reports of reliable narrators that are different from other scholars.
5. He knew the hadith and he considered it to be genuine, but he forgot it.
6. He did not know what the hadith means.
7. He believed that what his opponent used as proof from the hadith is a misconstruction.
8. He believed that the interpretation conflicts with something else that shows that the intent is other than what his opponent says.
9. He believed that the hadith is contravened by something that indicates that it is weak, or it is abrogated, or its meaning is figurative—if it is subject to being taken figuratively

and reassigned a different meaning by something accepted as valid by consensus, like a Quranic verse, another hadith, or scholarly consensus.
10. He believed that the hadith opposes something that proves that it is weak, abrogated, or reassigned a figurative meaning while other scholars did not share his view. Or [he held that] the category of the thing mentioned in the hadith is in opposition to something [else], or it is really not in opposition to anything, but is weightier [than the other report].

Ibn Taymiyah considers all ten of these causes for abandoning acting on the Prophetic hadiths to be valid excuses for the Imams in spite of the fact that he does not personally believe that anyone should abandon acting on any hadith, if it is sound, for any excuse due to his own orientation as a Hanbali. He says in defence of the Imams:

> *So, if it is presumed that any of this has issued from some of the notable personages among the scholars praised by the Ummah—in spite of being far-fetched and non-existent—one of them would only be prompted to do so by one of these causes. And if it had happened, it would not damage their leading status in the least.*

He also says:

> *Because for a surety, we do not believe that infallibility is a quality of any people [other than the Prophets]. On the contrary, we consider sin to be possible for them. And we have hope for them [to enter Paradise], in spite of that, due to what Allah ﷻ has specially distinguished them with of righteous deeds, exalted*

states, and that they did not persist upon sin. But they are not higher in rank than the Companions.

He says in his *Majmu'at al-Fatawa, Kitab at-Tasawwuf* p. 27, while speaking about some of the renowned Sufis, like Abu 'Abd Al-Rahman Al-Sulami:

And those who are regarded in the Ummah as having a tongue of broad truthfulness to the extent that he is commended and praised among the overwhelming majorities of the different classes of the Ummah, these are the Imams of right guidance and the lamps of the starless night. And their mistakes are few with comparison to their correct opinions. And most of them (i.e. their mistakes) result in the areas of ijtihad wherein they are pardoned while they are those who follow knowledge and justice. So they are far from ignorance and arbitrary action, and [far from] following conjecture and what souls lust for.

In this book, Ibn Taymiyah presents detailed arguments and examples to support his conclusions. And in the last portion of the book, he exhaustively speaks about the impermissibility of attaching sin to those with valid excuses and the prohibition against cursing the specific sinner for doing something for which the Prophet cursed people. He speaks about the impact of the threat of punishment on believers mentioned in hadiths for certain sins, and he enters into a polemic with those who argue that the prohibition of the sin can be established from such reports, but not the threat of punishment mentioned therein.

He also concludes in his discussion that it is also impermissible to ascribe sin even to the one who curses a specific person for committing a sin for which the Prophet ﷺ cursed people in general for doing. He says:

> *For I surely do not…deem it permitted to curse the one doing the act, and I do not permit cursing the one who curses the one doing the act. And I do not believe that the doer or the curser falls under the hadith concerning the threat. And I do not show harshness against the curser to the extent that those do who consider him as being subjected to the threat [of sin]. Rather, cursing him is undoubtedly one of the matters of disagreement in my view, and particularly in the general category of matters related to ijtihad. But I believe him to be in error in that regard, just as I believe the one who permits it to be in error…"*

This shows that Ibn Taymiyah was very careful about attaching negative labels to Muslims. Elsewhere he quotes the following hadiths that give credence to his stance:

> "The believer is not the disparager, not the curser, not the obscene (fahish), and not the foul-mouthed (badhi)." Tirmidhi reported it and said: A fair hadith (hasan).

> "It isn't proper for a truly sincere person (siddiq) to be one who curses (la'an)." Muslim reported it.

> "Verily the Disparagers (ta'anin) and the Cursers (la'anin) will be on the Day of Resurrection neither intercessors nor witnesses."

> "There is not a single man who curses anything that does not deserve it, except that the curse returns to him."[4]

This work of Ibn Taymiyah can be considered a study in Islamic Legal Theory *(Usul al-Fiqh)*. And the publication utilised for this translation is the 1418/1997 printing by Dar al-Kutub al-'Ilmiyah entitled *Raf' al-Malamm 'an al-I'immat al-A'lam*.

As for me, I have added additional footnotes to help aid the reader in understanding the text, prefacing each note by the word 'Translator.'

Our hope is that this rendering into English of *Removing Blame from the Distinguished Imams* is accepted solely for Allah's sake. And we hope that it benefits all those who read it.

Abdullah bin Hamid Ali

Introduction

All praise is due to Allah ﷻ for His favours. I testify that there is no god except Allah, alone. He has no partner in His Earth nor in His Heaven. And I testify that Muhammad is His slave, His messenger ﷺ, and the seal of His prophets. May Allah grant blessing everlasting to him, his family, and his companions until the day of meeting Him. And may He give total peace [to all of them].

Proceeding, [I declare that] it is a duty upon Muslims—after befriending Allah and His messenger ﷺ to befriend the believers—as the Quran has spoken of, especially the scholars who are the heirs of the prophets who Allah has placed at the rank of the stars. Guidance is taken from them in the darkest corners of land and sea. And the Muslims have unanimously agreed upon their right guidance and proficiency in knowledge.

Whereas, in every nation—before the advent of Muhammad —its scholars have been the worst of them except for the Muslims. For indeed *their* scholars are the best of them. And they are without doubt the successors to the Messenger ﷺ in his nation, and the revivers of what has died of his Sunnah. By them the Holy Book stands, and by it they stand. And the Holy Book speaks of them, and they speak of it.

And [I] let it be known that there is not one of the Imams who is universally accepted by the Ummah who intentionally contradicts the Messenger of Allah ﷺ in any of his Sunnah whether small or large. For they surely agree with certainty upon the obligation of following the Messenger ﷺ and upon the fact that every person has statements that can be accepted and [others that] can be rejected; contrary to [the case of] Allah's Messenger ﷺ. However, when a statement of one of them is found that a sound hadith contradicts, there must be an excuse in their abandonment of it. And all [legitimate] excuses are of three classifications: *The first of them*: is his belief that the Prophet ﷺ did not say it. *The second*: is his belief that particular issue was not intended by that statement. *And the third:* is his belief that ruling is abrogated."

The First Cause

He was unaware of the hadith

Whomever the hadith hasn't reached isn't burdened to know what it necessitates. And if it hasn't reached him—while he has taken a view about that issue that accords with the outward meaning of a verse, [or] with another hadith, [or] in accord with legal analogy (*qiyas*), or in accord with the rule of presumption (*istishab*)—it (i.e. the view) might agree with that hadith at times, and it might contradict it at others. This cause is the major reason for most statements of the Salaf that conflicted with some of the hadiths. For surely none of the Imams encompassed knowledge of all of the hadiths of Allah's messenger .

And the Prophet ﷺ used to relate [teachings], offer legal opinions (*yufti*), give legal verdicts (*yaqdi*), or he would do something and someone who was present would hear or see him, and then those—or one of them—would proclaim that [thing] to whoever they would run into [later]. Then the knowledge of that would reach whomever Allah willed of the scholars from the Sahabah, the Tabi'in, and those after them. Then in another sitting he might relate [a teaching], offer a legal opinion, give a legal verdict, or do something and some of those who were absent from that [earlier] sitting would witness it, and then they would proclaim it to whomever they could. Thereafter, these would have knowledge of what those did not have. And those would have knowledge of what these did not have. The scholars of the Sahabah and those after them gain distinction over one another by the scope and quality of knowledge of it [they possessed]. As for one of them encompassing all of the hadiths of the Messenger of Allah ﷺ, it is impossible for one to ever claim such a thing.

Consider [all of] that with regard to the Rightly Guided Caliphs who are the most knowledgeable of this Ummah regarding the affairs of Allah's Messenger ﷺ, his Sunnah, and his situations, especially [Abu Bakr] al-Siddiq ؓ who never left his company as either a resident or during travel. Rather, he was with him most of the time to the point that he would spend the night with him in conversation about the affairs of the Muslims. Likewise was 'Umar ؓ. For surely the Messenger of Allah ﷺ would often say: "I, Abu Bakr, and 'Umar entered…" And, "I, Abu Bakr, and 'Umar went out…" Despite that, when Abu Bakr ؓ was asked about the inheritance [that should be given] to the grandmother [of a dead person], he said:

> *There is no entitlement for you in the Book of Allah. And I do not know of any entitlement for you in the Sunnah of Allah's messenger ﷺ. But, I will ask the people (i.e. the learned).*

So, he asked them. And Al-Mughira b. Shu'bah and Muhammad b. Maslamah stood up and bore witness that the Prophet ﷺ gave her 1/6th [of the inheritance].[5] 'Umran b. Husain also related this Sunnah.

These three [men] were not equal to Abu Bakr and the other Caliphs [in knowledge]. But they were distinguished by having knowledge of *this* Sunnah whose application the Ummah has agreed upon.

∾

Similar was 'Umar ﷺ. He did not know the Sunnah of asking permission (*isti'dhan*)⁶ until Abu Musa Al-Ash'ari ﷺ informed him and asked the Ansar to bear witness, while 'Umar ﷺ was more knowledgeable than those who related to him this Sunnah.

'Umar ﷺ also did not know that a woman is to inherit from the blood-wit (*diyah*) of her husband. Rather, he held the view that the blood-wit belongs to the male agnates (*'aqilah*) until Al-Dahhak b. Sufyan Al-Kilabi ﷺ, one of those who governed some of the nomadic tribes for Allah's Messenger ﷺ, wrote to him informing him that Allah's Messenger ﷺ gave a portion of the inheritance to the wife of Ashyam Al-Dibabi ﷺ from the blood-wit of her husband.⁷ When he heard this he abandoned his opinion because of that. He said, "If we had not heard of this, we would have judged differently."

He also did not know the ruling about the Zoroastrians (*Majus*) regarding the payment of tribute (*jizyah*) until 'Abd Al-Rahman b. 'Awf ﷺ informed him that the Messenger of Allah ﷺ said, "Initiate with them the Sunnah of the People of the Book."⁸

And when 'Umar ﷺ came to Sargh⁹ and it reached him that the plague was in Sham, he consulted the first Emigrants (*Muhajirun*) who were with him, then [he consulted] the Ansar, and then the Muslims of the Conquest. So, each one offered to him their view, and no one reported a Sunnah until 'Abd Al-Rahman b. 'Awf came ﷺ. Then he told him of the Sunnah of Allah's Messenger ﷺ regarding the plague, and that he said:

> *When it falls upon a land while you are in it, do not go out taking flight from it. And when you hear of it in a land, do not go to it.*¹⁰

He and Ibn 'Abbas ﷺ discussed the matter of the one who has doubt [about the number of units prayed] in his Salat. But the Sunnah about that did not reach him until 'Abd Al-Rahman b. 'Awf said on the authority of the Prophet ﷺ, "He should cast off the doubt, and then build on what he is certain of."[11]

And once while on a journey a wind was stirred, and then he begun to say, "Who can relate to us something about the wind?" Abu Hurayrah ﷺ said:

> *Then he reached me and I was in the back of the crowd. So I urged my riding beast until I caught up to him, and then I related to him what the Prophet ﷺ ordered anytime the wind blows.*[12]

So these are occasions of which 'Umar ﷺ did not know [something] until another person proclaimed it to him. And there are other occasions when nothing of the Sunnah reached him, and he issued a verdict, or gave a legal opinion without that [Sunnah], like when he issued a verdict about the blood-wit given for [the loss of] fingers in that they differ according to their uses [so there is a different cost to be paid for each respective finger lost]. Abu Musa and Ibn 'Abbas ﷺ who were much lesser than him in knowledge—had knowledge that the Prophet ﷺ said, "This and this [finger] are equal."[13] That is, the thumb and the pinky. Later, this Sunnah reached Mu'awiyah ﷺ during his reign, and he judged according to it. And the Muslims found no escape from following that. But that was not a flaw in 'Umar's regard ﷺ in that the hadith did not reach him.

Similarly, he, as well as his son, 'Abdullah b. 'Umar, and other people of virtue ﷺ used to forbid the Hajj pilgrim (*muhrim*) from wearing perfume before adorning the pilgrim garb (*ihram*), and before going to Mecca after stoning the pillar of Al-'Aqabah. But the hadith of 'Aishah ﷺ did not reach them:

> *I placed perfume on the Messenger of Allah ﷺ for his pilgrim garb before he adorned the garb, and for its removal before he circumambulated the House.*[14]

He also used to order the one wearing the leather socks (khuff) to wipe over it until he took it off without setting a time limit. And a faction of the Salaf followed him in that. But the hadiths concerning the time limit, which are sound (sahih) and known by some of those who were not their equal in knowledge, did not reach them. And that has been related about the Prophet ﷺ from a variety of sound channels.[15]

And similar was the case with 'Uthman ﷺ. He did not have knowledge that the widow is to spend her mourning period in the house of the deceased husband until Al-Furay'ah bt. Malik, the sister of Abu Sa'id Al-Khudri ﷺ, related to him her case when her husband widowed her, and that the Prophet ﷺ said to her, "Remain in your home until the decree reaches its appointed term."[16] Then 'Uthman adopted it ﷺ.

And, once the meat of a hunted animal was given to him as a gift, which was hunted for him specifically. So he got the urge to eat it until 'Ali ﷺ informed him[17] that the Prophet ﷺ returned meat that was given to him as a gift[18].

Likewise, was the case of 'Ali ﷺ who said:

> *Whenever I heard a teaching from Allah's Messenger ﷺ, Allah benefited me with what He willed to benefit me from it. And when others related something to me, I would ask him to swear. So when he swore, I would*

believe him. And Abu Bakr related [things] to me—
and Abu Bakr spoke the truth...

Then he mentioned the famous hadith of Salat al-Tawbah[19].

He ('Ali), Ibn 'Abbas, and others ﷺ gave a legal opinion that when the widowed woman is pregnant, she is to spend her waiting period [for mourning] according to the longest of the two periods.[20] But the Sunnah of Allah's messenger ﷺ did not reach them with reference to Subay'ah Al-Aslamiyyah ﷺ when her husband, Sa'd b. Khawlah, widowed her whereas the Prophet ﷺ passed the legal opinion that her waiting period [before remarrying] is until she gives birth.[21]

He ('Ali), Zayd, Ibn 'Umar, and others ﷺ gave a legal opinion about the woman whose dower is on consignment (*mufawwadah*) that when her husband dies, she receives no dower [from his inheritance]. But the Sunnah of Allah's Messenger ﷺ did not reach them about Barwa' bt. Washiq ﷺ.

So this is a broad chapter. What is reported of it about the Companions of Allah's messenger ﷺ reaches a very high number. As for what is reported of it from other than them, it cannot be enumerated. For surely, it is in the thousands.

These were the most knowledgeable of the Ummah, the most learned of it, and its most pious and virtuous. Those after them are more imperfect. And to lack in knowledge of some of the Sunnah for those [who come after] is more suiting. That does not require any explanation.

He who believes that every sound hadith (sahih) has reached each one of the Imams or a specific Imam is disgracefully and utterly mistaken. So let no one say, "The hadiths were documented and collected. So [for one of them] to lack knowledge of [any of] them—while this is the case—is remotely unlikely, because these famous compilations about the Sunnahs were collected only after the passing of the exemplary Imams—may Allah show them mercy." Despite this fact, it is not possible to claim that all the hadiths of Allah's Messenger ﷺ are thoroughly encompassed in these limited collections. Then, if we were to presume that all the hadiths of Allah's Messenger ﷺ are encompassed in them, then all that is contained in books is not known to the scholar. And that [complete comprehension] does not occur to almost anyone. Rather, a man might have numerous collections while he does not even encompass what they contain. Rather, those who were before the compiling of these collections were more knowledgeable of the Sunnah than those who came later by much, because much of what reached them and was accepted as being sound to them may only reach us from one who is unknown, or with a severed chain. Or, it might not reach us in its totality. In addition, their collections were their breasts that contain multiple times as much as the written compilations may contain. And this is a matter that whoever knows the case has no doubt about.

And let no one say, "Whoever does not know all the hadiths is not a *mujtahid*", because if it was stipulated that a *mujtahid* must know all that the Prophet ﷺ said and did ﷺ with regard to what relates to law (*ahkam*), then there would be no *mujtahid* in the Ummah according to this [standard in history]. Rather, the required amount [of knowledge] for the scholar is for him to know the greater majority of that [information] and most of it in such a way that only a small degree of detail is unknown to him. So it might happen that he will then go against that small degree [he lacks] of detail that happens to be absent from what has reached him.

The Second Cause

He was aware of the hadith, but it wasn't sound in his view

[This happens] either because he is the [only] one who relates it, or the one who relates it to the one who relates it, or [because] another transmitter in the chain is unknown to him, is suspect, or has a faulty memory.

Or [it might happen] because it (the report) did not reach him with a connected chain (*musnad*). That is, [its chain is] severed (*munqati'*). Or he did memorise the exact words of the hadith in spite of the fact that with that hadith, reliable transmitters related it to other than him with a connected chain while the other person knew the one who was unknown to the former scholar to be reliable. Or, transmitters other than those devalued (*majruhin*) by him happened to relate it. Or, [it may happen that] a chain different from the one disrupted has connected it, and some of the hadith masters (*huffaz*) have precisely memorised the words of the hadith. Or, that [first] version has auxiliary and additional reports (*shawahid*[22] and *mutaba'at*[23]) that clarify its soundness.

And this [sort of miscalculation] happens quite often too. It happens amongst the Tabi'in and the Tabi' Al-Tabi'in until [the time of] the famous Imams after them more than it occurs during the first generation or much of the first part [of the first generation]. For surely the hadiths had already become widespread and well known. However, they used to reach many of the scholars from weak chains while it had reached others from sound chains other than these chains. Therefore, they would become a proof from this [weak] chain in spite of the fact that they did not reach those [scholars] who opposed them based on the other chain. Consequently, in the statements of more than one of the Imams were [comments alluding to] them suspending their personal views when in conflict with a hadith on the condition of its soundness. One (of them) might say, "My view in this issue is *such and such*. And a hadith has been related in its regard with *such and such*. So if it is *sahih* (sound), then it is my view."

The Third Cause

He believes the hadith presented by those differing with him is weak

[This happens] in spite of it being reported from another chain of narration. And he takes the same stance even if his [view] is correct, [or] if another's view [is the correct one], or if both of them are correct as is [the case] with those who say, "Every *mujtahid* is correct." And that [cause] branches out into a number of subdivisions:

One of them: is when one of those relating the hadith believes that it is weak while the other believes it to be acceptable. And the knowledge of transmitters is a broad science. So, the one who believes it to be weak might be correct due to him knowing [that it contains] a weakening factor (*sabab jarih*).

Contrarily, correctness might be with the other due to his knowledge that [weakening factor suggested] cannot devalue [the transmitter] either because such a factor cannot weaken [a transmitter] or because he (the transmitter) has an excuse [or quality] that makes devaluation impossible in his regard. This is also a broad chapter. The scholars of hadith transmitters and their conditions, in that regard, have points where they agree and where they disagree similar to what the case is with other scholars in their special disciplines.

Another subcategory of this third cause: is when the one relating hadith has two states: a state of integrity (*istiqama*) and a state of confusion (*idtirab*), like if he happened to mix up variant reports, or if his books happened to be consumed in a fire. Whatever he relates in the state of integrity is [considered] sound. And whatever he relates in the state of confusion is [considered] weak. Later, he might not even know which of the two categories the hadith falls under (accepted or rejected). But others [might] know that it is part of what he related while in the state of integrity.

Another subcategory: is when the one relating the hadith forgets the hadith. Then he does not recall it afterwards, or he denies ever having related it [to others] while believing that this [particular occurrence] is a weakness ('illa) that requires one to abandon the hadith, while others might hold the view that this [lack of recollection] is a factor that grants soundness to it. The case [of this argument against accepting a hadith] is well known.[24]

Another subcategory: is when many of the scholars of the Hijaz hold the view that the hadith of an Iraqi or Shami cannot be used as proof if it doesn't have an origin in the Hijaz whereas one of them said:

> *Place the hadiths of the people of Iraq at the rank of the hadiths of the People of the Book. Do not confirm them as true. And do not declare them to be false.*[25]

And it was said to another, "Is Sufyan from Mansur from Ibrahim from 'Alqamah from 'Abd Allah b. Mas'ud authoritative?" He replied, "If it does not have an origin in the Hijaz, then, no!" And this is due to their belief that the People of the Hijaz perfected the Sunnah, so not a single part of it escaped them, and that [as for] the hadiths of the Iraqis, confusion (*idtirab*) occurred in them that required one to remain neutral in their regard.

Some of the Iraqi's hold the view that the hadiths of the

Shami's cannot constitute a proof, even though most of the scholars (*nas*) abandon ascribing weakness [to reports] because of this. So whenever the chain is good (*jayyid*), the hadith is a proof whether the hadith is from the Hijaz, Iraq, Sham, or from any other place.[26] And Abu Dawud Al-Sijistani—may Allah show him mercy—composed a book about the unique reports about the Sunnah (*mafarid*) reported by the peoples of the various metropolises. In it he elucidated the Sunnahs that were unique to every metropolis that are not found with a connected chain with others, like [the unique reports from] Medina, Mecca, Ta'if, Damascus, Hims, Kufa, Basra, and elsewhere. And there are subcategories [to this cause] other than these stated.

The Forth Cause

He stipulates conditions for the reports of reliable narrators that are different from other scholars

[This is] Like when some of them stipulate that one weigh the hadith against the Kitab and the Sunnah [to avoid contradiction][27]. It is also like when others stipulate that the one relating the hadith must be a jurist (*faqih*) whenever it (the hadith) conflicts with a legal analogy done with the well-established rulings of Islam (*qiyas al-usul*).[28]

It is also like when some of them stipulate that [knowledge of] the hadith should be widespread and pervasive when it relates to something that should be common need [for all] to know (*ma ta'ummu bihi al-balwa*)[29]. And there are other examples [that fall under this cause] that can be drawn from the appropriate sources (*mawadi'*).

The Fifth Cause

He knew the hadith, considered it to be genuine, but forgot it

This is found with respect to the Kitab and the Sunnah, like the well-known hadith from 'Umar ؓ wherein he was asked about the man who is stricken with major ritual impurity (*janabah*) during travel, and then does not find water. He said, "He is not to pray until he finds water." Then 'Ammar b. Yasir ؓ said:

> O Commander of the Faithful! Do you not recall when you and I were amongst the camels and we became ritually unclean? I wallowed as riding beasts do.[30] As for you, you did not pray. So I mentioned that to the Prophet ﷺ and he said: "To do as you did is sufficient."

So, he touched the Earth with his hands, and wiped his face and hands with them. Then 'Umar said to him, "Fear Allah, O 'Ammar!" He said, "If you would like, I will not relate it." He (Umar) said, "Nay! We will burden you with the responsibility of what you have undertaken."[31]

So this is a Sunnah that 'Umar ؓ witnessed, and then forgot

to the point that he offered a legal opinion contrary to it. And 'Ammar ؓ reminded him, but he ('Umar) did not remember. And he did not believe 'Ammar was lying. On the contrary, he ordered him to relate it. And clearer than this is that he ('Umar) delivered a public address to the people, and then said:

> *No man shall pay a dower higher than the one given to the Prophet's wives and his daughters* ؓ *except that I will return it!*

Then a woman said to him, "O Commander of the Faithful! Why do you deny us something that Allah has given to us?" Then she read, *'And if you desire to replace a wife with another wife, and you have given one of them a heap of gold, then do not take anything from it.'* [Al-Nisa: 20] So 'Umar retracted his statement due to her report, although he had committed the verse to memory. But he had forgotten it until reminded.

Similar to this, is what was related when 'Ali reminded Al-Zubayr—on the Day of the Camel—of something that Allah's Messenger enjoined upon them. So he remembered it and then left the fighting.[32] Such happened frequently among the Salaf and the Khalaf.[33]

The Sixth Cause

He did not know what the hadith meant

[In other words, a scholar might oppose a hadith] sometimes due to the wording in the hadith being strange to him, words like, '*Muzabanah*'³⁴, '*Mukhabarah*'³⁵, '*Muhaqalah*'³⁶, '*Mulamasah*'³⁷, '*Munabadhah*'³⁸, '*Gharar*'³⁹, or other strange words that the scholars might differ over their interpretations.

And [included are things] like the prophetic hadith (*marfu'*), "There is no divorce or emancipation under *ighlaq*."⁴⁰ For, verily, they interpreted *ighlaq* to mean *ikrah* (coercion). But those who differ do not know this explanation.

Sometimes [a scholar might oppose a hadith] because its meaning in his dialect (*lughah*) and his customary usage ('*urf*) is not what it means in the Prophet's . So he might construe it according to what he understands in his dialect on that basis. But the rule is to apply the primary meanings [of words until impossible to apply] (*al-asl baqa al-lugha*).

Similarly, some of them heard reports (*athar*) about the license given for [drinking] steeped-dates (*nabidh*). So they thought it was one of the kinds of intoxicants (*muskir*), since it was their dialectical understanding (*lughah*).⁴¹ But it was actu-

41

ally nothing more than dates tossed [in water] for soaking in order to sweeten the water before it becomes intense [enough to produce drunkenness] [*yashtaddu*]. For surely it has been explained in a number of sound hadiths.

Add to that, they heard the word '*khamr*' (wine) in the Kitab and the Sunnah, and believed that is was specifically the fermented juice of grapes based on the fact that it means that in the language [42], even though there are sound hadiths that have come explaining that '*khamr*' is a name for every drink producing drunkenness.[43]

At times [one might not understand the meaning of the hadith], because the word might be a homonym (*mushtarak*)[44], an ambiguous expression (*mujmal*)[45], or rotating between literal (*haqiqa*) and figurative (*majaz*). So one will construe it according to what one deems it to be closest to, even though the intent may be the other [meaning]. This is how a group of the Companions in the beginning construed [Allah's saying], '*The white thread and the black thread*'[46] as a reference to a rope.[47] Likewise, others construed His (Allah) statement ﷻ '*Then wipe your faces and your hands.*' [Al-Mai'dah 5: 6]—to mean [to wipe] the hand to the underarm pit.[48]

And at times [one might not understand the meaning] due to the fact that the indication cannot be clearly applied (*khafiyya*). For, verily, the different types of indications from statements are very broad [in scope]. People differ in superiority with respect to grasping them and comprehending the different forms of speech according to [degree of] the blessings (*ni'mah*) given by The One True God (Allah) and His divine gifts (*muwahib*).

Then a person might happen to know it as a general expression, but does not understand that this particular meaning [being applied in the new instance] falls into that general meaning. Then he might understand it sometimes, and then forget it later. This is also a very broad topic. Only Allah fully grasps it.

Additionally, a person might err, and adopt an understanding from certain comments in the Arabic language, [the language] with which Allah's messenger was sent ﷺ, things that are not understood by the natives of the language.[49] [But, it might be understood only by the interpreter's in his mother tongue, which is not Arabic].

The Seventh Cause

He believes that his opponent misconstrues the hadith

The difference between this [individual] and the one before him [in the sixth cause] is that the latter did not know the basis of the [hadith's] interpretation [in that way], while the former knew the basis of the interpretation. But he also believes that it is incorrect due to there being a source [of legislation] that invalidates this interpretation. [He feels that way] whether that [interpretation] is correct or incorrect [in fact].

[This is] like when one believes that the general expression that has some of its constituents excluded (*'amm makhsus*) is not authoritative.[50] Or [like believing] that the base understanding of an expression (*mafhum*) has no authority,[51] or that the general expression [in a scriptural text] that is attached to a specific occasion of revelation (*'umum warid 'ala sabab*) is applied specifically to its occasion.[52] It is also like when an unqualified verbal command (*amr mujarrad*) does not produce obligation, or it does not necessitate immediate compliance (*fawr*).[53]

It is also like when the word defined by the definite article (*al* = i.e. 'the') does not express generality,[54] or when negated actions[55] neither result in the negation of the persons they refer to (*dhawatuha*) nor all the rulings connected with them.⁵⁶

A similar example is [like] when an expression with pursuant applicability (*muqtada*) does not express generality, to the point that he (the scholar) will not claim any point of generality in concealed subjects (*mudmarat*) or unapparent meanings (*ma'ani*). And [there are] other things besides those that would take too much time to mention.⁵⁷

For verily in half of the Science of Legal Theory (*Usul al-Fiqh*), the areas of disagreement fall under this topic (linguistic studies) despite the fact that the bare principle sources (*usul mujarrada*)⁵⁸ do not cover all of the linguistic indications around which there exists disagreement.

Also under this section [of disagreement] are 'the particulars classified under the different categories of linguistic indications (*afrad ajnas al-dalalat*).' [The question is asked] Are they in that category or not? [This is] like for one to believe that a specific word is ambiguous (*mujmal*) due to it being a homonym (*mushtarak*) void of an [exterior base] indication that would isolate any one of its two meanings, or [is it under] another [category]?

The Eighth Cause

He believes that the interpretation conflicts with something else that shows that the intent is other than what his opponent says

[This is] like when a general expression is contravened by one that is specific,[59] [when] one that is unqualified (*mutlaq*) is contravened by one that is qualified (*muqayyad*),[60] [when] an unqualified verbal command [is contravened] by something that negates obligation [from it],[61] or [when] an outward meaning [of a word is contravened] by something that indicates that the word is understood figuratively.[62] And add to that, all the other forms of contradictions. This is also a broad topic. For surely [the examples of] contradiction occurring between expressions in statements and giving superiority to some over others is a vast sea.

The Ninth Cause

He believes that the hadith is contravened by something that indicates that it is weak, or it is abrogated, or its meaning is figurative—if it is subject to being taken figuratively and reassigned a different meaning by something accepted as valid by consensus, like a Quranic verse, another hadith, or scholarly consensus

This (cause) takes two forms:

One of them: is for one to believe that this point of contradiction outweighs [the hadith] as a whole. So one of the three [probabilities mentioned] must be applied without applying any one of them specifically.

And at times: one of the points is specifically applied by him (the scholar) while believing that it (the hadith) is abrogated or applied in its figurative sense. Then, one might err about [the claim of] abrogation and believe that the *latter* ruling [that abrogates] is the *earlier* ruling.

One might also err in applying the figurative meaning [to the hadith] by construing the hadith according to a meaning that its wording cannot convey, or there may be something opposing it (i.e. the scholar's figurative interpretation). And if it (the factor) conflicts with it (the hadith) as a whole, the opposing factor may not be indicative [of what he says], and the conflicting hadith may not be as strong as the first one in either its chain (*isnad*) or text (*matn*). In this instance, the causes mentioned prior become manifest, and others manifest in the first hadith.

And scholarly consensus (*ijma'*) claimed in most cases is no more than [the result of] not knowing anyone who is in opposition. And we have found among the distinguished personages of the scholars those who have adopted views about things while they are founded upon [them] not knowing anyone who is in opposition [to the view], in spite of the fact that the apparent meanings of the proofs they present necessitate the opposite [of what they say about them]. Nevertheless, it is not possible for the scholar to introduce a statement when he does not know of anyone who says it while knowing that other scholars have stated the opposite of it to the extent that there are those among them who attach a condition to their proclamation and say, "If there is a consensus on the issue, it is deserving of being followed. Otherwise, the ruling in my view is *such and such*." That is also like the one who says, "I do not know of anyone who has permitted the testimony of the slave." But the acceptance of it is recorded from 'Ali, Anas, Shurayh, and others ﷺ. And another says, "They have unanimously agreed that the one who is partially emancipated does not inherit." But, his inheritance [from another] is recorded from 'Ali and Ibn Mas'ud ﷺ. And there exists a fair (*hasan*) hadith with respect to it from the Prophet[63] ﷺ. Another says, "I do not know of anyone who has made sending prayers on the Prophet ﷺ compulsory in Salat." But, the obligation of it is recorded from Abu Ja'far Al-Baqir.[64] That is because the extent [of knowledge] of many of the scholars is that they knew the opinion of the people of knowledge they came across in their countries while they did not know the opinions of a number of groups other than them.

Similarly, we find that many of those of the early period (*mu-*

taqaddimin) knew no more than the view of the Medinites and the Kufans. And many of those of the latter days (*muta'akhkhirin*) knew no more than the view of two or three of the Imams who are followed, and they did not go beyond that. For, verily one, in such a person's view would contradict a consensus, only because he did not know anyone who said such a thing, while the opposite of it (the strange view) is what regularly struck his ears. So this individual cannot yield to a hadith that contradicts this [view of his scholar] due to his fear that this *might* be in contradiction to consensus (*ijma'*), or due to his *belief* that it is contradictory to consensus. And consensus is the greatest of all proofs. This is the excuse of many people in much of what they forsake. Some of them are actually pardoned in it while others of them are pardoned in it [outwardly] but not pardoned in actuality. Thus is the case of many of the causes [mentioned] before and after [this one].

The Tenth Cause

He believes that the hadith opposes what proves that it is weak, abrogated, or reassigned a figurative meaning while other scholars do not share his view. Or the category of what is mentioned in the hadith is in opposition to something, or it is really not in opposition to anything. Rather, it is weightier.

[This is] like the opposition of many of the Kufans[65] to sound hadiths due to [their conflict with] the outward indication of the [verses of the] Quran, and their belief that the outward indication of the Quran —the general expressions (*'umum*) and others like it—is to be placed before the explicit text of the hadith. Then, one might believe what is not *outward* to be outward due to the variety of meanings implied by the statement [while he knows of only one or two]. Due to this, they rejected the hadith related about [accepting] the '*[testimony of the single] witness along with his oath*' (*shahid wa yamin*) in spite of the fact that others know that there is nothing in the outward indications in the Quran that say anything that forbids passing a judgment on the premise of [the testimony of] a single witness with an oath.[66] And if such a thing did exist, then the Sunnah is the explainer of the Quran in their [own] view. Shafi'i has well known comments about this rule. And Ahmad has, with respect to it, his famous Treatise (*Risalah*), which is a rebuttal against those who claim that it is enough to consider only the outward meanings expressed in the Quran without needing any explanation from the Sunnah of Allah's messenger ﷺ. And he outlined in it proofs, but this place is too small to mention any of it.

One of the consequences of that would be: the rejection of the hadith that gives specification to the general expressions of the Kitab, [and rejecting the hadith] giving qualification to the unqualified expression or one that contains an addition [to what is in the Quran]. And the belief of those who say this is that the addition to the text is the same as qualifying the unqualified (*mutlaq*), and abrogation (*naskh*), and [they believe] that giving specification to the general is [also] abrogation. [This prior position is] also like when a group of the Medinites oppose the sound hadiths with the actions of the *Scholars* of Medina based on the fact that they (the scholars of Medina) are in agreement about being at variance with the report. So their consensus is a proof placed over the report.[67]

An example of this is how they oppose the hadiths related to 'the option [of completing or canceling a transaction as long as one is] in the sitting' (*khiyar al-majlis*) based upon this source [of law],[68] even though, most of the scholars (*nas*) may at times affirm that the Medinites have undoubtedly differed over this issue and that if they had all agreed,[69] while others differed with them, the authority would be in the report [since this does not constitute consensus of the scholars of Medina].

[These two prior arguments are] also like the opposition [offered] by *scholars* from the two [holy] sanctuaries (i.e. Mecca and Medina) to some hadiths [that they oppose][70] with clear legal analogy (*qiyas jali*) based upon the fact that the legal maxims that are agreed upon (*qawa'id kulliyyah*) cannot be rendered void by the like of this report [that they oppose]. And there are other types of conflict other than those, that exist whether they are [deemed] correct or incorrect.

So these ten causes [for abandoning hadiths] are clear. And regarding a number of hadiths, it is possible that the scholar may have a [valid] proof in giving up acting according to hadiths that we have not become acquainted with. For surely the ways of grasping knowledge are many. And we have not become acquainted with all of what is in the minds (*bawatin*) of the scholars.[71] And a scholar may at times produce his proof, while [at others] he might not produce it. When he produces it, it might reach us, just as it might not reach us. And when it has reached us, we might grasp his point in using it as proof, or we might not grasp [it]. And that is whether the proof is correct in itself or not.

However, in spite of us considering this possible, it is not permissible for us to swerve from a view whose proof has appeared through a sound hadith that a faction of the people of knowledge have agreed with. [We may not swerve from the hadith] to take a contradictory view that a scholar has stated with whom it is possible that he may have that by which he can repel this (hadith) proof, even if he is more knowledgeable [than those who support the hadith].[72]

This is because error strikes the opinions of the scholars more than they strike the scriptural proofs (*adilla shar'iyyah*). For indeed the scriptural proofs are Allah's evidence against all of His slaves. But the same cannot be said for the opinion of the scholar.[73] And it is impossible for the scriptural proof to be an error if another [scriptural or legal] proof is not in opposition to it, while the same cannot be said of the opinion of a scholar (i.e. the opinion of a scholar can always be opposed and considered erroneous as long as it is not agreed upon). If it was permissible to act upon this proposition of possibility (*tajwiz*) there would remain in our hands nothing of the proofs wherewith the like of this is possible.[74] However, the aim is [to establish] that one may in himself be pardoned for his abandonment of it. And we are pardoned for our abandonment of this abandonment.⁷⁵ Allah ﷻ says, '*This is a nation. It has already passed. For it is what it earned. And for you is what you earn. And you will not be asked about what they used to do*' (Baqarah: 134). And Allah ﷻ says, '*Then if you dispute with one another in a thing, refer it back to Allah and the Messenger if you do believe in Allah and the Last Day*' (Nisa: 59).

And no one can oppose the sound hadith from the Prophet ﷺ with the view of any one of the people, as Ibn 'Abbas ؓ said to a man who asked him about an issue and he answered him with a hadith. The man said to him, "Abu Bakr and 'Umar said…" So Ibn 'Abbas said:

> *Stones from Heaven are on the verge of descending upon you! I say: The Messenger of Allah ﷺ says. And you all say: Abu Bakr and 'Umar said*!!!⁷⁶

And if the abandonment [of acting on the hadith] is the result of some of these causes, then when a sound hadith authorises, prohibits, or contains a ruling, it is not permissible to believe that the scholar who abandons it—among those whom we have described the reasons for their abandonment—will be punished for permitting a prohibited act, forbidding a permissible act, or judging by other than what Allah has revealed. Likewise, if the hadith contains a threat about an action in the form of a curse, anger, punishment, or the like, then it is not permissible to say that that scholar who permitted this or did it falls under that threat. This is from what we don't know [there to be] among the Ummah any disagreement except for a trifle related about some of the Mu'tazilah of Baghdad, like Bishr Al-Murisi⁷⁷ and the likes of him, who claimed that the *mujtahid* who errs would be punished for his mistake.

This is because attaching the threat to the one who does the forbidden is conditioned upon him knowing that it has been deemed forbidden, or upon him coming to know that it is deemed forbidden. For surely, one who has grown up in a nomadic village (*badiyah*) or is new to Islam who then does one of the prohibited acts while not knowing that it is deemed forbidden, is not in sin and is not given the determined penalty, even if he does not rely upon a scriptural proof in considering it to be permissible. So, whoever has not been reached by the hadith giving the prohibition and who relies upon a scriptural proof for the permissibility is more deserving of being pardoned. Therefore, such an individual [scholar] is rewarded and worthy of praise because of his *ijtihad*. Allah ﷻ says,

'And [mention] David and Solomon, when they judged concerning the field— when the sheep of a people overran it [at night], and We were witness to their judgment; And we gave understanding of it (i.e. the case) to Solomon, and to each [of them] We gave judgment and knowledge.' Anbiya: 78-79.

So, Solomon specifically was characterised with understanding. But He extolled both of them with judgment and knowledge. And in the *Two Sahihs* from 'Amr b. Al-'Aas ﷺ the Prophet ﷺ said:

> When the judge exerts himself (ijtahada) and is correct, he has two rewards. And when he exerts himself and errs, he has one reward.

So it becomes plain that the *mujtahid* in spite of his mistake has one reward. And that is due to his *ijtihad* while his mistake is forgiven for him, because achieving correctness in all particular cases of judgments is impossible or extremely difficult. And Allah ﷻ has said, '*He has not made any difficulty on you in religion*' (Hajj: 78). And He ﷻ said, '*Allah desires ease with you. And He does not desire difficulty with you*' (Baqarah: 185). And in the *Two Sahihs* [it is mentioned] about the Prophet ﷺ that he said to his Companions in the year of the *Battle of the Ditch*, "Let no one pray, unless it is in Banu Qurayza" Then Salat caught them on the way. So some of them said, "We will only pray in Banu Qurayza." Others of them said, "He didn't mean that from us."

So they prayed on the way, and he did not criticise any of the two factions. The first [faction] adhered to the general purport of the statement and made the case (*sura*) of missing [the prayer] enter into the generality [of his statement]. And the others, there was with them proof that necessitated excluding this case from the generality. For, verily, the aim was to make haste to those that the Prophet ﷺ laid siege to.[78] And it is an issue that the jurists have a well-known disagreement about [in their circles]: [That issue is] 'Can general expressions be made specific through legal analogy?'[79] In spite of this, those who prayed on the way were more correct in acting.

Similarly, Bilal ؓ when he sold two *Sa'*s[80] of dry dates for one *Sa'*, the Prophet ﷺ ordered him to return it.[81] And he did not assign to that the ruling of devouring interest (*riba*) that pertains to declaring one to be immoral (*fasiq*), [being a subject of] the [Prophet's] curse (*la'n*), and being shown harshness (*taghliz*) due to him lacking knowledge of its status in being prohibited.

Similar are 'Adi b. Hatim and a group of the Companions ؓ when they believed that His saying—High is He, '*...until the white thread becomes distinct to you from the black thread...*' (Baqarah: 178)—meant '*the white and black ropes.*' So one of them would place at his pillow two halters— one white and one black, and eat until one of them would become distinguished from the other. So the Prophet ﷺ said to 'Adi, "Surely your pillow is broad then. It is merely the whiteness of the day and the blackness of the night."[82] So, he alluded to his misunderstanding of the meaning of the words. And he did not assign to that act the blame assigned to the one who breaks fast during Ramadan, even though it is one of the gravest of major sins.

[This is] contrary to those who offered a legal opinion (*fatwa*)—to the one who had the head wound (*mashjuj*) during the cold—about the obligation of performing *ghusl* (the ritual shower). So he made *ghusl* and died. For surely he ﷺ said,

> They killed him. May Allah kill them! Do they not ask when they do not know? The only cure for incompetence (*'ayy*) is asking.[83]

For indeed they erred without [having the qualifications for] *ijtihad*, since they were not among the people of knowledge.[84]

Similarly, he did not oblige against Usama b. Zayd any supervised retaliation (*qawad*), the payment of blood money (*diyah*) or expiation (*kaffarah*) when he killed the one who said, "*Laa ilaha ila Allah*" during the raid on *Al-Huraqat*.[85]

For, surely, he had believed that it was permissible to kill him based upon the fact that the surrender (*Islam*) was not sincere (*sahih*) in spite of the fact that his murder was forbidden. The Salaf and the overwhelming majority of the jurists acted in accord with that [ruling], whereas whatever the [Muslim] rebels (*Ahl al-Baghy*) deemed permissible from the blood of (*Ahl al-'Adl*) the just folk [who fought against them] with a reasonable *mis*interpretation (*ta'wil sa'igh*), it (i.e. the lives lost) would not be indemnified with blood retribution, blood money, or expiation, even though killing and fighting them (i.e. against the people of justice) was forbidden.

Our mention of this condition for attaching the threat [to the doer] does not have to be mentioned in every address because the knowledge of it is firmly established in hearts. Likewise, the promise of good (*wa'd*) for action is premised upon doing the act solely for Allah and the act not being invalidated because of apostasy. But this condition is not mentioned in every hadith that contains a promise of good.

So in spite of presuming the presence of the thing that would necessitate [applying] the threat, the ruling [of sin] is undoubtedly lifted due to something that bars [it from being applied] (*mani'*). And things that bar attaching the threat are various.

One of them is: repentance (*tawbah*). *Another is:* asking forgiveness (*istighfar*). Others are: the good deeds that erase bad deeds (*al-hasanat al-mahiyatu li al-sayyi'at*). Others are: the tribulations experienced of the mundane world and its afflictions (*bala al-dunya wa masa'ibuha*) Another is: the intercession of the one whose intercession is accepted (*shafa'tu shafi' muta'*) And another is: the mercy of the Most Merciful of those who show mercy (*rahmatu Arham al-Rahimin*).

So, when all of these causes [for abandoning the hadith] are absent— and they will never [all] be absent except with regard to he who wreaks havoc, rebels, and strays from Allah the straying of the camel from its owner—then, that is when the threat will be attached to *the scholar*. That is because the true nature of the threat is to clarify that this deed is a cause for this punishment. So, the prohibition of the act and its ugliness are deduced from that.

As for if there is an individual within whom this cause is present, whereby it is necessary that the thing resulting from it occur (i.e. punishment or rebuke), then this would be absolutely invalid, due to the happening of that result being premised upon the existence of the condition and the cessation of everything that bars (*mawani'*).[86] To clarify that is to say that whoever abandons acting according to a hadith, it (i.e. the abandonment) can only fall into [one of] three different divisions:

Firstly, it is a permissible abandonment by the agreement of the Muslims (i.e. the scholars), like the abandonment of the one that the hadith never reached who was not negligent in the search [for hadith evidence] in spite of his need to give a legal opinion (*fatwa*) or judgment (*hukm*), as we mentioned about the Rightly Guided Caliphs and others—may Allah be pleased with them; [Under] this [division], a Muslim has no doubt about the person involved in it in that nothing of the shame of abandonment attaches to him.

Secondly, the abandonment might be impermissible. This is

something that almost never issues from the Imams—God willing. However, what might be feared about some of the scholars is that a person might be unfit to comprehend the ruling of that issue [he speaks of]. So, he will make a statement without mentioning the reasons for the statement, even though he has looked deeply into the matter and done an exhaustive study of it; Or he will fall short in seeking proof and then make a statement before the study is complete and full, in spite of clinging to proof [he might have]; Or [it might be that] a social custom (*'adah*) will influence him, or [he may have] an aim (*gharad*) that prevents him from doing an exhaustive study in order to look at what opposes what he has. And if he stated a view premised on merely *ijtihad* or *istidlal*,[87] then the end that the *ijtihad* must reach may not be fully encompassed by the *mujtahid*. Consequently, the scholars were afraid of the like of this out of fear that the [person's qualification for] *ijtihad* considered is found only in that specific issue.

So, these are sins. However, attaching the [the threat of] punishment for the sin to its doer is done to the one who has not repented, even though asking forgiveness, good treatment [of others], enduring tribulation, intercession, and mercy might erase them. And this does not apply to the one whose lust overwhelms him and leads to his downfall whereas he knows that it is falsehood; nor to those who speak in certain terms about the correctness of a statement or the incorrectness of it without knowing the proofs for that view whether in negation or in confirmation [of it]. For a surety these two are in the Fire as the Prophet ﷺ said:

> *The judges are three. Two judges are in the Fire. And one judge is in the Garden. So, as for he who is the Garden, he is a man who knew the truth and gave a verdict according to it. And as for the two who are in the Fire, they are a man who gave a verdict for the people while lacking knowledge, and a man who knew the truth but gave a verdict contrary to it.*[88]

And those who offer legal opinions (*Muftis*) are similar. However, attaching the threat to a specific person also has things that bar it [from applying to him] as we have explained. So, if it is presumed that any of this has issued from some of the notable personages among the scholars praised by the Ummah—in spite of being farfetched and non-existent—one of them would only be prompted to do so by one of these causes. And if it had happened, it would not damage their leading status in the least. Because for a surety, we do not believe that infallibility is a quality of any people [other than the Prophets]. On the contrary, we consider sin to be possible for them. And we have hope for them [to enter Paradise]—in spite of that—due to what Allah has specially distinguished them with of righteous deeds, exalted states, and that they did not persist upon sin. But they are not higher in rank than the Companions .

Such is to be the [the manner of] discussion about them with respect to what they deduced of legal opinions (fatwas), verdicts (*qadaya*), and the internecine strife (*dima*) that happened between them as well as others. Then, while knowing that the one who forsakes [acting on the hadith] is described as being forgiven—by all means—that he is rewarded, it does not prevent *us* from following the sound hadiths that we do not know to have an opposing [proof] that would negate them, and [it does not prevent us] from believing that it is compulsory for the Ummah to act upon them as well as proclaiming them. This is something scholars do not differ about.

Then, hadiths divide into those whose indications are decisive (*qat'iyyah*) in the way they were transmitted (*sanad*) and [decisive] in the meanings they convey (*matn*). It is what we are certain that Allah's Messenger ﷺ actually said, and what we are certain of that he meant by it in this form [of expression]. [Hadiths also divide into] those whose indications are quasi-explicit (*zahirah*) but indecisive (*ghayru qat'iyyah*) [in both the way they are transmitted and in the clarity of their meanings].

As for the first [kind of hadith], it is compulsory to believe what it obligates of knowledge and action. This is from what there is no difference of opinion about between the scholars as a whole. They might differ over some reports only [in matters like]: Is it indisputably transmitted or is it disputable? Is it decisive in indication or is it indecisive? [This is] like their difference over the non-concurrent report of the person or people (*khabar al-wahid*) whom the Ummah has received with acceptance and confidence or that [report] that it has agreed to act upon. According to the masses of the jurists and most of the dialectical theologians (*mutakallimin*) it produces definitive knowledge (*'ilm*). But, factions of the dialectical theologians adopted the view that it does not produce it.[89] Similar is the report related from a number of [different] channels confirming one another coming from a specific group of people. It might produce certainty (*'ilm yaqini*) to he who knows those channels, [knows] of the condition of those reporters, and [knows] of indications and added characteristics that surround the report, even if the knowledge of that did not occur to the one who does not share with him in that.

Because of this, [to] the critical hadith masters who were profoundly rooted in the knowledge of it—may Allah show them mercy, complete certainty about reports might occur to them, even though other scholars might not think them to be genuine and not know that they are [actually] genuine. The source of this is that the report that produces certainty produces it from the *numerousness* of those reporting—at times; From the *characteristics* of those reporting—at other times; from the *reporting* itself—at others; from the *reporter's comprehension* of it in itself—at others, and from the *matter reported*—at other times.

So how many a small number there are whose reports have produced definitive knowledge (*'ilm*), due to the religiosity they possess and the perfect retention, which grant us security from them lying and erring, while multiples of that number other than them, their reports might not produce definitive knowledge! This is the truth wherein there is no doubt. And it is the view of the overwhelming majority of jurists, hadith specialists, and factions of the dialectical theologians. And factions of the dialectical theologians and some jurists adopted the view that every number whose report has produced definitive knowledge in one case, the report equal to this number also produces [it] in every case.[90] This is absolutely false! But this is not the place to clarify that.

We have not mentioned how contexts (*qara'in*) outside of those who report influence the knowledge of the report, because those contexts might produce definitive knowledge [by themselves] if they are stripped away from the report. And if they (contexts) happen to produce definitive knowledge by themselves, they are not made subordinate to the report by any means, in the same way that the report is not made subordinate to them. Rather, each of them is a path to definitive knowledge—at times, and [a path] to non-definitive knowledge (*zann*)—at other times, if either we combine the element in each of them that produces definitive knowledge by itself, or we combine the element producing definitive knowledge from one of them with the element producing non-definitive knowledge from the other.

And one who happens to be more knowledgeable of the reports might decisively declare the reports to be genuine, while one who is not his equal might not decisively declare the genuineness of the same reports. At times they differ [even] about the [level of] explicitness of the indication due to their difference over whether that hadith is [fully] explicit in indication (*nass*) or quasi-explicit in indication (*zahir*). And if it happens to be quasi-explicit in indication, [they would differ even more about] does it contain something that negates the probable meaning (*ihtimal*) that is discarded (*marjuh*) or does it not? This is also a vast topic.

Then, some folk among the scholars might decisively declare the indication of some hadiths to be what others might not declare them to decisively indicate, either because of their knowledge that the hadith can only be construed according to that meaning, or due to their knowledge that the other meaning is forbidden for the hadith to be construed according to it, or due to other proofs that produce unequivocal meaning.

As for the second division [of hadiths]—it is those that are *quasi-explicit in indication* [of authenticity and meaning]. Such must be acted upon in the scriptural rulings of law (*fiqh*) by the agreement of the scholars who are given consideration. If such happens to include a rational judgment (*hukm 'ilmi*), like the threat [of Fire] or its like, they differ about it. Factions of the jurists (*fuqaha*) adopted the view that the report of the trustworthy individual, whenever it includes a threat against an action, it must be acted upon in declaring that act to be forbidden. But it is not applied with respect to the threat unless it happens to be indisputably authentic (*qat'i*). The same stands if the text happens to be indisputably authentic, while the expressional indication is merely quasi-explicit (*zahir*). Accordingly, they construed the statement of 'Aisha ﷺ to the wife of Abu Ishaq Al-Sabi'i, "Proclaim to Zayd b. Arqam that he has nullified his striving (*jihad*) with Allah's Messenger ﷺ unless he repents."⁹¹

They said:

> So 'Aisha ﷺ mentioned the threat because she had knowledge of it. And we acted upon her report in determining the prohibition (*tahrim*), even though we do not attest to the threat because the hadith has been

> *established with us only through a disputably authentic report (khabar wahid)."*

And the proof with these [scholars] is that the threat [of punishment] is one of the definitive matters (*umur 'ilmiyya*). Such can only be determined by things that produce definitive knowledge (*'ilm*). In addition, when the ruling of an action is the result of *ijtihad*, the threat does not attach to the one who does it.

So, according to the view of these [scholars]: the hadiths mentioning threats [of punishment] are used as proof in determining the prohibited nature of actions under all circumstances. But the threat [itself] cannot be attached to them unless the indication [via transmission] is indisputable. For example, most scholars present as proof the modes of Quranic recitation (*qira'at*) that have been confirmed to be sound from some of the Companions—may Allah be pleased with them—in spite of the fact that they are not in the Official Copy (*Mushaf*) of 'Uthman ﷺ. For indeed they contain both *applicable laws* and knowledge in spite of being the sound report of only one individual.

So, they used them as proof in establishing the practice [contained therein], but they did not confirm them to be Quran, because they (the modes) are among the definitive matters, which can only be confirmed with definitive knowledge (*yaqin*). And most of the jurists (*fuqaha*)—in addition to the populous among the Salaf—adopted the view that these hadiths are a proof in all that they contain with regard to the threat. For indeed the Companions of Allah's messenger ﷺ and the Successors (*Tabi'un*) after them continued to confirm the threat by this hadith, just as they confirmed the *laws inferred* by them. And they would explicitly state that the threat mentioned in them attaches to the doer [of those actions] as a whole. And this is prominently known about them through their hadiths and legal opinions (*fatawa*).

That is because the threat is part of the sum total of the rulings deduced from scripture that are confirmed sometimes through expressions whose meanings are quasi-explicit and at other times through expressions whose meanings are unequivocal. For surely complete certainty is not a thing desired in confirming the soundness of the threat. Rather, what is desired is [no more than] the belief [in the occurrence of the threat] that falls within the sphere of certainty or near certainty (*zann ghalib*). And this is the same that is desired with regard to the rulings that pertain to practice. And there is no difference between a person's belief that Allah has made this forbidden and has threatened its doer with the unspecified punishment and the belief that Allah forbade it *or* threatened against doing it with a specified punishment. In other words, each of them is giving news about Allah . So, just as giving news about Him of the first with an unqualified proof (*mutlaq al-dalil*) is permissible, likewise, it is permissible to give news about Him of the second. Rather, if one was to say "Applying them concerning the threat is given greater priority", it would be correct.

Due to this, they used to tolerate the chains of narration [of hadiths] that encourage *toward good* and discourage *from evil* (*targhib wa tarhib*). But, they were not tolerant with regard to [the weakness of] chains of the hadiths from which laws were deduced (*ahkam*), since believing in the threat induces souls to the abandonment [of evil].[92]

༄

Then, if that threat happens to be true, the person is saved. And if the threat does not happen to be true—i.e. the punishment for the act is lighter than that threat—it will not harm the person to be mistaken in his belief about the added punishment, if he abandons that act. That is because if he happens to believe the punishment is light, he might also err. In the same way, if he does not believe in that added degree [in punishment] while negating or confirming [it], he might as well err. Then, this erring as a result might make him deem the act to be light, thereby he would fall into it, and then deserve the added punishment if it happens to be confirmed, or [at the least] the cause for him to deserve that might exist in him. Hence, the error in belief according to both presumptions—i.e. the presumption of believing the threat and the presumption of not *believing* it—is equal. And salvation from the punishment from the regard of the presumption of believing the threat is closer. So, this presumption would be more fitting.

And because of this proof, the community of the scholars declared the evidence forbidding [an act] to be weightier than the evidence permitting [it].[93] And many of the jurists followed the path of caution in many rulings on this premise. As for observing caution about the act, it is like [other acts] whose goodness is unanimously agreed upon between all rational beings as a whole. So, when his fear of error—through negating the belief in the threat—is parallel with his fear in the absence of this belief, the evidence obliging one to believe in it and the salvation resulting from believing in it remain two proofs free of anyone who is in opposition.

And none can say "The lack of *decisive* proof about the threat is a proof of its absence, similar to when there is a lack of the decisive concurrent report (*mutawatir*) as pertains to the Quranic readings added to what is in the Official Compilation (*Mushaf*) [It is not given the ruling of being the Quran]," [This cannot be said] because a lack of proof [for something] does not indicate [anything about] the matter being pointed to. [So it is an inconsistent analogy].

And whoever unequivocally declares the negation of anything falling within the realm of matters determined by reason due to the absence of decisive proof of their existence—as is the approach of a faction of the dialectical theologians, he is erring clearly and manifestly. However, when we know that the existence of something that makes it binding that the evidence exists while knowing that the evidence does not exist, we unequivocally declare the non-existence of the thing whose presence is obligated, since the absence of the obligating factor (*lazim*) is a proof of the non-existence of the thing obligated (*malzum*).

And we have known that the incentives to transmit the Book of Allah and His religion are abundant. For, verily it is not permissible for the Ummah to conceal [the report] whose transmission the people require [to be taken] as a universally acknowledged proof. So, since a sixth prayer (*salat*) has not been reported universally nor has another *sura*, we know for a certainty that such a thing does not exist.

And the subject of the threat is not a part of this topic. For indeed it is not necessary in every threat against a misdeed that it be transmitted via a decisive concurrent report (*mutawatir*), just as such a thing is not required with regard to [establishing] the ruling of that act.

So, it has been established that the hadiths that contain threats must be acted upon in what they necessitate with the belief that the doer of that act is threatened with that particular threat. However, attaching the threat to him rests upon conditions. And that [attachment] has things that bar (*mawani'*) it [from being attached to him].

This rule will clarify itself through examples:

One of them: is what has been soundly confirmed about the Prophet that he said:

> May Allah curse the devourer of interest, the one who gives it to him to devour, the two who witness it, and the one who writes it down.

And it has been soundly confirmed about him from more than one channel that he said to the one who sold two *sa's* for one *sa'* hand by hand (i.e. without delay of exchange), "Aw! (It is) the essence of interest (*riba*)." Just as he said, "Wheat for wheat is interest unless it is *ha* and *ha*… (to the end of the hadith)."[94]

And this necessitates the entrance of the two types of interest—the interest of *increase* and the interest of *delay*—into the hadith. Then, there are those who the Prophet's statement has reached , "Interest is merely with respect to the delay."⁹⁵ [Upon hearing this] they considered it permissible to sell two *sa's* for one *sa'* hand to hand, people like Ibn 'Abbas ؓ and his companions, Abu Al-Sha'tha, 'Ata, Tawus, Sa'id b. Jubayr, 'Ikrimah, and others amongst the chief personalities of the Meccans who were the best of the Ummah in knowledge and practice. *In spite of this*, it is not permissible for a Muslim to believe about any one of them in particular or those who took them as a model—in a manner that it is permissible to follow them—that the curse of the one who devours interest attaches to them, because they did that while innocently misinterpreting [the issue] in a manner that is easy to swallow as a whole.

Similar is what has been conveyed about a faction of the virtuous personages from the Medinites regarding anal-sex (*ityan al-mahash*) in spite of what Abu Dawud relates about the Prophet ﷺ saying, "Whoever comes to a woman from her backside, he is an unbeliever in what has been revealed to Muhammad ﷺ!!!"⁹⁶

It has also been confirmed about him ﷺ that he cursed ten with regard to wine: The squeezer of the wine (*'asir*), the presser of it (*mu'tasir*), and the drinker of it…*to the end of the hadith*.⁹⁷ And it has been confirmed about him from different channels that he said, "Every drink that intoxicates is wine." And he said, "Every intoxicant is wine."⁹⁸

And 'Umar ؓ spoke on his pulpit between the Emigrants (*Muhajirun*) and the Helpers (*Ansar*), and said, "Wine is what mixes with the mind."

Allah revealed the prohibition of wine. And the occasion of its revelation was [related to] what they used to drink in Medina. And they had no other drink except date-wine (*fadikh*). They had nothing of the wine of grapes. And men from the virtuous personages of the Ummah—in knowledge and practice—among the Kufans used to believe that there was no wine but that of grapes, and that all besides grapes and dates, none of its steeped brands are forbidden except for the extent that produces intoxication.[99] And they would drink what they believed permissible.

So, it is not permissible to say, "Surely these are included under the threat" due to the excuse they had by which they justified it, or due to other things that bar (*mawani'*) it [from being attached to them]. It is also not permissible to say, "Surely the drink they drunk is not the type of wine the drinker is cursed for", because the thing that brought about the general statement inescapably must enter under it in spite of there being no wine [produced] from grapes in Medina [at the time of the revelation]. Then, the Prophet ﷺ cursed the seller of wine.[100] And some of the Companions sold wine until it reached 'Umar ﷺ. So he said:

> *May Allah curse So and So! Does he not know that Allah's messenger ﷺ said: "May Allah curse the Jews! Fats were forbidden on them. So they dressed them up and sold them, and devoured their costs!*[101]

The *Companion* did not know that the sell of it was forbidden. And 'Umar's knowledge of his lack of knowledge did not prevent him from explaining the recompense of this sin, in order that he and others would abandon it after achieving knowledge of it.

And Allah's messenger ﷺ cursed the squeezer and the presser. And many of the jurists permit for a person to squeeze grapes for other than himself, even if he knows that the intention of the one who is to take the squeezed grapes is to use it for wine.[102] This explicitly shows that the squeezer is cursed in spite of knowing that the one with an excuse, the ruling is placed behind him because of something that bars (*mani'*) it [from attaching to him].

Likewise is the curse of the woman who adds false hair to another (*wasilah*) as well as the one who is adorned with false hair (*mawsulah*) in a number of sound hadiths. However, there are those of the jurists who merely consider it to be disliked.[103]

The Prophet ﷺ said, "Verily he who drinks in vessels of silver takes into his belly nothing more than the fire of Hell (*Jahannam*)."[104] But, there are those amongst jurists who dislike it with the dislike meant [only] to remove guilt (*kirahat tanzih*) [through its abandonment].

Similar is his saying ﷺ, "When two Muslims encounter one another with their swords, the murderer and the one murdered are both in the Fire."[105] It must be acted upon in prohibiting fighting between Muslims unrightfully. Then, we assuredly know that the People of the [Battle of the] Camel (*Jamal*)[106] and [The Battle of] *Siffin*[107] are not in the Fire, since they have an excuse and a validly understandable misinterpretation (*ta'wil*) that led to their fighting; in addition to good deeds that bar the necessary result from doing its work.[108]

And he ﷺ said in the sound hadith:

> *There are three that Allah will neither speak to nor look at them on the Day of Resurrection. He will also not purify them, and they will have a grievous penalty: A man possessing a surplus of water who denies it the wayfarer. Allah will say to him: "Today I will deny you my surplus (fadl) just as you denied the surplus of what your hands played no part in." [The other is] a man who pledged allegiance to an Imam who he only pledged allegiance to because of a worldly matter: If he gives it to him, he is satisfied. And if he is not given it, he gets angry. And [third is] a man who swears [that he has a right] on a commodity after 'Asr while lying: He has surely been given because of it (i.e. his lying) more than what he was given [by the owner of the commodity].*"[109]

So, this is a grave threat to whomever denies the surplus of his water, in spite of the fact that a faction of the scholars permit for a person to deny the surplus of his water.

This disagreement does not prevent us from believing that this is prohibited while presenting the hadith as proof. And the existence of the hadith does not prevent us from believing that the one who reasonably misinterprets [it] is pardoned for [doing] that. So, the threat does not attach to him. He ﷺ said, "May Allah curse the one who gives license [to remarry] (*muhallil*) and the one given license (*muhallal lahu*)."[110]

[The '*muhallil*'—the one who gives license—is the man who marries another man's ex-wife, who the latter divorced three times, with the objective of making her lawful for her ex-husband. The '*muhallal lahu*' is the one who she is made lawful for].

It is a sound hadith. It has been related about Allah's messenger—may Allah bless and grant him peace—from more than one channel, and from his Companions as well ﷺ in spite of the fact that a faction of the scholars considered the marriage of the licensor (*muhallil*) to be valid under all circumstances.[111] And among them are those who declared it to be valid when it is not stipulated in the contract. They have well-known justifications in that [in the circles of the People of Knowledge].

For indeed the result of applying the universal legal principles (*qiyas al-usul*) in the first case would be that marriage is not voided by conditions, just as it is not voided by lacking knowledge of one of the items of exchange [in the marriage].[112] The result of applying the universal legal principles in the second case would be that contracts stripped of any condition attached [to them] do not change the rulings applied to contracts. Add to all of that, this hadith did not reach the one who adopted this view. This is what is apparent. For surely their writings of earlier times (*kutubuhum al-mutaqaddimah*) did not include it. And if it had reached them, they would have mentioned it while adhering to it (i.e. the hadith), or they would have responded to it. Or, [perhaps] they interpreted it [differently], or believed it to be abrogated, or they had [evidence of] what was in contradiction to it. So, we know that [with] the like of these [individuals], this threat does not reach them if one [of them] had done *tahlil* (permitting the marriage of one's irrevocably divorced ex-wife through a mock-marriage with a different man) while believing its permissibility in this manner. But, that does not keep us from knowing that *tahlil* is a cause for this threat, even though it is lacking with regard to some individuals due to the loss of a condition or the existence of something that bars it.

Similar is Mu'awiyah's claim of blood ties (*istilhaq*) with Ziyad, his father's son born on the bed of Harith b. Kaladah ※, since Abu Sufyan used to say that without doubt he was from his seed. [He used to say this] in spite of the fact that Allah's messenger ※ said, "Whoever makes a claim to other than his father while knowing that he is not his father, Paradise is forbidden for him."[113]

And he said:

> Whoever makes a claim to other than his father or claims clientage to other than his clients (*mawali*), then on him is the curse of Allah, the angels, and all of humanity. Allah will neither accept from him an exchange nor indemnity.[114]

[It is] a sound hadith. He ruled that the child belongs to the bed it was born in]. And it is one of the agreed upon rulings.[115]

So, we know that whoever is ascribed to other than the father, who is the owner of the bed, enters into the Messenger's comments ※ in spite of the fact that it is not permissible for anyone other than the Companions—or even the Companions themselves—to be specified and said of them, "Surely, this threat is attached to him," because of the possibility that the verdict of Allah's messenger ※ did not reach them that the child belongs to the bed. And [it is because of the possibility that] they believed that Abu Sufyan was the one who impregnated Sumaiyah, the mother of Ziyad. For surely this ruling might escape many people, especially prior to the spread of the Sunnah, in spite of the fact that the norm in the Pre-Islamic Era (*Jahiliyah*) was this way, or due to factors other than that, which prevent the necessary result of the threat from doing its job [because] of good deeds that efface bad deeds and other virtues.

This is a broad topic. For surely all matters forbidden by the Kitab and the Sunnah fall under it whenever some of the Imams have not been reached by the hadiths that forbid [things] and then consider them to be permitted; Likewise [is the case whenever] other proofs they have considered to be weightier than them in their view oppose those hadiths while exerting *ijtihad* in declaring that [thing] to be weightier according to their rationale and knowledge.[116]

For surely declaring a thing to be forbidden has [various] rulings [that take the form] of the ascription of sinfulness (*ta'thim*), blameworthiness (*dhamm*), [warranting] punishment (*'uqubah*), [accusation of] open defiance (*fisq*), and other than that. However, it has conditions (*shurut*) and inhibitors (*mawani'*).

The prohibition might be confirmed [in a report] while these rulings [inferred from it] might be unconfirmed due to the lack of its prerequisite, or the presence of what bars it, or the prohibition [might] happen to be removed with reference to that person despite being applied to others. And we repeated the comments merely because the scholars (*nas*) have two views in this issue:

One of them—which happens to be the view of the generality of the Salaf and the jurists (*fuqaha*)—is that Allah's ruling is one, and that whoever contradicts it with a reasonable *ijtihad* (*sa'igh*) is in error, forgiven, and rewarded [altogether].

So, according to this [view], that act done by the *muta'auwil* (one who innocently misconstrues the command) is essentially forbidden. However, the effect of the prohibition (i.e. punishment) does not become a consequence of it due to Allah's pardoning of him. For surely He only burdens a soul with its capacity [to bear].

The second [view]: is that it (i.e. the action), in his regard, is not forbidden, because the evidence indicating prohibition has not reached him, even though it is forbidden with regard to others. Consequently, the actual motion of that person is not forbidden.[117] And the difference is slight (*mutaqarib*). It is akin to a difference in the way of expressing [the same thing].

So, this is what can be said about the hadiths containing threats whenever you come across a matter of disagreement, since the scholars are unanimous about presenting them (i.e. the hadiths) as proofs in prohibiting the act, which is the object of the threat whether it (i.e. the issue) is a point of agreement or [one of] disagreement.

Rather, their greatest need is to use them as proof in the areas where disagreement is found (*mawarid al-khilaf*). However, they differed about seeking proof by them for the threat when they do not definitively indicate (*qat'iyah*) what we have mentioned.

So, if it is said, "Then why did you not say that the hadiths containing threats do not deal with the points of disagreement, but they deal with the points of agreement? And [why not say that] every action whose doer is cursed or threatened with wrath or punishment because of it, it is construed to be an action whose inviolable nature is agreed upon in order that some *mujtahids* do not enter into the threat when he does what he believes to be permissible. Rather, [why not say that] the one who believes it goes farther than the doer, since he is the one who orders him to do the action. Consequently, the threat of the curse or wrath is attached to him by way of necessity."

[If they say this] We would say: The answer is from [a number of] ways:

One of them: is that the category of prohibition (*tahrim*) will either be confirmed in the case of disagreement or it will not be. So, if it is never confirmed in the case of disagreement, it is a necessary result that it not be forbidden except for what is unanimously declared to be forbidden. For surely everything over which difference exists about its prohibition will be lawful (*halal*). But this is contrary to the consensus of the Ummah. And it is known to be invalid by necessity from the religion of Islam.[118]

And if it (i.e. the prohibition) happens to be confirmed—even if, in form, then the *mujtahid* who deems that forbidden act to be permissible, the blameworthiness of one who declares the forbidden to be permissible or does it either attaches to him along with its punishment, or it does not.

Then, if it is said, "Indeed it attaches to him" or it is said, "Indeed it does not attach to him", then *the same can be said* about the prohibition confirmed in the hadith containing the threat by consensus (*ittifaq*) as well as the threat confirmed in the point of disagreement according to what we have mentioned at detail. Rather, the threat was directed only at the doer. And the punishment of the one declaring the forbidden permissible fundamentally is greater than the punishment of the one doing it while not believing [its permissibility]. So, if it is possible for the prohibition to be confirmed in the case of disagreement while the punishment for that authorisation of the forbidden is not attached to the *mujtahid* who deems [it] permissible due to his being pardoned in it, then for the threat of that act to not be attached to the doer is more deserving and more fitting. And just as it is not a necessary result that the *mujtahid* falls under the ruling of this prohibition—as relates to blameworthiness, punishment, and other than that, it is also not a necessary result that he enter under its ruling as relates to the threat, since the threat is nothing more than a kind of blameworthiness and punishment. So, if it is possible for him to enter under this category, then whatever is a response to some of its subcategories is also a response to the rest.

And making a distinction between a small amount of blame and a lot of it or the gravity of the punishment and the lightness of it is of no avail. For verily what is warned against with regard to a little bit of blame and punishment in this place is just like what is warned against with regard to a lot of it. For, surely the *mujtahid* neither a little of that nor a lot of it attaches to him. Rather the opposite, the reward attaches to him.

The Second: is that the fact of the ruling of the act being agreed upon or differed about are matters outside [of the essence] of the act and its characteristics. They are merely matters that are added according to what appears to some scholars due to the lack of knowledge [of others].

And the general expression, if something specific is intended by it, it is necessary to present an evidence that indicates the specification— either attached with the address—according to those who do not deem it allowable [for the Messenger] to delay the clarification [of a thing], or [while] granting space in its delay until the time of need [for clarification] —according to the overwhelming majority.[119]

And there is no doubt that those addressed with this [unqualified expression] during the time of Allah's messenger ﷺ were in need of knowing the ruling of the address. So, if what was intended by the general expression in cursing the devourer of interest, the *muhallil*, and others, whose prohibition are unanimously agreed upon—and that [consensus] is only known after the Prophet's death ﷺ while he has spoken to the Ummah about all the individual elements of that general [expression], he would have delayed the clarification of his words until he spoke to the entire Ummah about all of its individual elements. But this is not possible.

The Third: is that these words, the Ummah were addressed by them only so that they would know the forbidden, and then they would avoid it, use it as support for their consensus, and they would present it as proof in their disputes.

So, if the form [of sin] intended had been only what they had unanimously agreed upon, the knowledge of *the sin* intended would have been premised upon consensus. Consequently, it would not be valid to present it as proof before the consensus. Then, there would be no supporting text (*mustanad*) for the consensus because the supporting text for consensus must precede it. And, it is impossible for it to come after it. For, surely it leads to circular reasoning (*dawr*), which is fallacious. For verily [with] the People of Consensus (scholars) at that moment, it would not be possible for them to find proof in the hadith in any form until they knew that it (i.e. the form) is what was intended. And they would not know it to be intended until they have all agreed. So, them finding proof (*istidlal*) would become premised on the consensus [occurring] before it, and the consensus would be premised on locating proof before it when the hadith happened to be their support. Then, a thing would become premised on itself. So, its existence would be impossible. And it would not be a proof in the case of the disagreement, because it was not found.

And this is rendering the hadith inoperable from indicating the [desired] ruling in the case of agreement *and* disagreement. And that necessitates that nothing of the [scriptural] texts that contain an element emphasising the gravity of the act produces for us prohibition against that act. But this is absolutely invalid.

The Forth: is that this necessitates that nothing of these hadiths are to be presented as proof until there is knowledge that the Ummah has unanimously agreed upon this [particular] form [of threat]. Consequently, [for] the Pioneers (*al-Sadr al-Awwal*), it would not have been permissible for them to present them as proof. Furthermore, it would not be permissible for those who heard them from the mouth of Allah's messenger ﷺ to present them as proof. And it would be a duty upon the person—when he hears the like of this hadith, and finds that many of the scholars have acted upon it while not knowing any one opposing it—to not act upon it until he looks to find out if there is anyone in any region of the Earth who opposes it. In addition, it would not be permissible for him to present consensus as a proof in a matter after a full search.

Hence, presenting the hadith of Allah's messenger ﷺ would be invalidated by the mere disagreement of one of the *mujtahids*. So, the statement of one individual would invalidate the words of Allah's messenger ﷺ while his agreement would establish the truth of the statement of Allah's messenger ﷺ.

And when that one individual errs, his mistake would invalidate the words of Allah's messenger ﷺ. But, all of this is invalid by necessity. For surely if it is said: It is only presented as proof after knowledge of the consensus [occurs], [and when] the indication (*dalalah*) of the texts becomes premised on consensus (*ijma'*). But it (as an argument) is contrary to consensus. In such a case, there would remain no indication in the texts. For surely the only thing considered would be consensus—while the text would be ineffective.

And if it is said, "It can be presented as proof, since the existence of disagreement is not known," then the statement of one individual from the Ummah would invalidate the meaning of the text. And this too is contrary to consensus. Its invalidity is known by necessity from the religion of Islam.

The Fifth: is that it is either stipulated that the entire Ummah's belief in the prohibition enters into the all-inclusiveness of the address or the belief of the scholars [in that] is deemed sufficient.

So if the first thing is true, it is not permissible to seek proof for the prohibition through the hadiths containing the threat until it is known that the entire Ummah—those growing up in the far away nomadic villages (*bawadi*) and those who have recently entered into Islam—all believe that this is forbidden. And this is something no Muslim says. Rather, not any rational person [says this]. For surely [obtaining] knowledge with this condition is practically impossible (*muta'adhdhir*).

And if it is said, "The belief of the scholars is deemed sufficient," it is said to him: You only stipulated the consensus of the scholars out of fear that the threat might include some of the *mujtahids* even if he happened to be in error. This in itself is found amongst those of the commoners who have not heard the evidence for the prohibition. For surely the danger of the curse involving this individual is like the danger of the curse involving this [other] individual.

And it does not save one from this being a necessary consequence (*ilzam*) to say, "That is one of the greatest figures of the Ummah and the virtuous among the truly sincere (*siddiqin*). And this is one of the less significant ones (*atraf*) of the Ummah and [one of] its commoners."

For, surely to make a distinction between the two of them in this manner does not prevent them from having a shared portion in this ruling. For verily Allah ﷻ—Just as He forgives the *mujtahid* when he errs, He forgives the ignorant when he errs when it is not possible for him to learn.[120] Rather, the harm (*mafsadah*) that results from one of the commoners doing a forbidden act whose inviolable state he did not know of and he was not able to know its inviolable state is far less than the harm that issues from some of the Imams declaring to be permissible what the Divine Law Giver (Allah) has deemed to be forbidden while not knowing of its inviolable state when it is not possible for him to know its inviolable state.

Due to this, it is said, "Beware of the scholar's slip! For verily if he slips, a [whole] world slips because of his slip!" Ibn 'Abbas ؓ said, "Woe to the scholar from followers!"

So, if this one is pardoned despite the greatness of the harm issuing from his act, then for the other to be pardoned despite the lightness of his act is more deserving.

Yes! They are different from another regard. It is that this one did *ijtihad* and spoke based on *ijtihad*. And he has through the dissemination of knowledge and revitalisation of the Sunnah *enough* [goodness] to engulf this harm. Allah has made a distinction between them from this regard. Then He rewarded the *mujtahid* for his *ijtihad*, and He rewarded the scholar for his knowledge a reward that that ignorant person did not share with him in. So, they share in the pardon, while not sharing (*muftariqani*) in the reward.

And for the punishment to fall upon one who is undeserving is impossible [according to scripture], whether he is of high importance (*jalil*) or low importance (*haqir*). So, it is a must to expel this impossible factor from the hadith such that it encompasses both divisions.

The Sixth: is that among the hadiths containing threats are those that are explicit in [including] the case (*sura*) of disagreement, like the curse applied to the *muhallal lahu* (i.e. the one whose irrevocably divorced ex-wife is made permissible for him by a mock marriage to another). For verily among the scholars are those who say that this [person] does not sin at all because he was not a chief element (*rukn*) in the initial contract by any means such that it can be said '*he is cursed*' due to his belief in the obligation of fulfilling the *tahlil* (i.e. his belief in the permissibility in the process of making his ex-wife lawful in marriage).

So, whoever believes that the marriage of the first [husband] is valid—even though the condition is null, while she is undoubtedly permissible for the second [husband]—he has stripped the second [husband] from sin.

Rather, the *muhallil* (i.e. the second husband who initiates the mock marriage) is similar. For, surely he is either cursed because of the *tahlil*, or only because of his belief in the obligation of fulfilling the condition attached to the contract, or because of both of them. So, if it happens to be the first or the third [case], the aim has been achieved.

But, if it happens to be the second [case], then this belief is the thing necessitating the curse whether there was a *tahlil* that occurred or one that did not occur. In that case, what is mentioned in the hadith would not be a cause for the curse. And the cause for the curse would not present itself to him. But such a thing is invalid.

Then, this individual who believes that it is compulsory to fulfill (the *tahlil*), if he is ignorant, there is no curse against him. And if he has knowledge that it is not compulsory, then it is impossible for him to believe the obligation [of doing so] unless he is spiting the Messenger ﷺ in which case he would be an unbeliever (*kafir*).

So, the meaning of the hadith would refer back to the curse of the unbelievers. And unbelief (*kufr*) has no special status in [us] raising objection to this particular ruling to the exclusion of others. So, this—being at the rank of one who says, "May Allah curse the one who attributes falsehood to the Messenger" ﷺ in his ruling by stipulating divorce in marriage—is invalid. Then, this statement (*kalam*) is general in both wording and meaning. And this is an absolute generalisation ('*umum mubtada*').[121]

[With] the like of this generalisation, it is not permissible to construe it to include rare cases (*suwar*), since the [meaning of the] statement would be rendered implausible and inapplicable (*luknatan wa 'iyyan*), as in the interpretation of the one who interprets his statement ﷺ, "Any woman who marries without the permission of her guardian, her marriage is void" to refer to the woman engaged in buying her freedom (*mukataba*).

To explain its peculiar nature is [to say] that the ignorant Muslim does not fall under the hadith. And [for] the learned Muslim, by the fact that this condition (marriage with the condition that the newly married wife be divorced) does not have to be fulfilled, one does not stipulate that he (the learned) believe in the obligation of fulfilling it unless he happens to be an unbeliever [since it is obviously unbinding to fulfil to the learned]. But the unbeliever does not get married in the way that Muslims get married unless he happens to be a hypocrite. And the occurrence of this marriage in this fashion is one of the rarest of rarities.

And if it was said that the like of this situation (*sura*) almost never appears to the mind of the one speaking, then the one making the comment would be speaking truthfully. And we have mentioned the abundant proofs elsewhere in that [in] this hadith, the *muhallil* who intentionally does it, even if he did not make it a condition is the one intended by it.

༄

Of like nature is the specific threat of the Curse, the Fire, and other things. It (i.e. the curse) has been stated explicitly (*mansus*) in different places along with disagreement about them, as in the hadith of Ibn 'Abbas ☙ from the Prophet ☙ who said, "May Allah curse those females who visit graves, those who take over them places of worship and lamps." Tirmidhi said, "(It is) A fair hadith (*hasan*)."[122] And [as for] a woman's visit [to graveyards], some *scholars* have given a license [for women] to do it, while others have considered it to be disliked, but did not declare it to be forbidden.[123]

And [another example is] the hadith of 'Uqba b. 'Amir ☙ from the Prophet ☙ who said, "May Allah curse those who come to women in their anuses (*mahashihinna*)."[124]

And [another example is] the hadith of Anas ☙ from the Prophet ☙ who said:

> *The jalib (one who tugs his goods to town to sell them) is guaranteed provision (marzuq), and the muhtakir (one who monopolises and holds on to needed goods until the market price rises) is cursed.*[125]

And already mentioned is the hadith:

> *The three who Allah will not speak to, will not look at them, will not purify them, and for them shall be a grievous penalty...*

[Another one of them included is the hadith about] he who

denies [to others] his surplus of water.

He has also cursed the seller of wine, even though some of those of the early days sold it.[126]

And it has been soundly confirmed that he said—may Allah bless and grant him peace, "Whoever drags his lower garment (*izar*) out of conceit, Allah will not look at him on the Day of Resurrection."[127] And he said:

> *There are three whom Allah will not speak to, will not look at, will not purify them, and they will have a grievous penalty: The one who trails his lower garment, the one who reminds of his charity to others (mannan), and the one who disposes of his commodity with the false oath.*[128]

[All of this is reported] in spite of the fact that a faction of the jurists say that the dragging and trailing [of the waistcloth] out of conceit is disliked, not forbidden.[129] Similar is his statement:

> *"May Allah curse the wasilah (woman who adds hair extensions) and the mawsulah (the one the hair is added to)."*

It is one of the soundest of hadiths[130] while there is a well-known disagreement about hair extensions (*wasl al-sha'r*). Likewise is his saying, "Verily the one who drinks in the vessels of silver crepitates in his stomach nothing more than the fire of Hell."[131] But among the scholars are those who do not deem that to be forbidden.

The Seventh [way of responding]: is [to say] that the thing obligating all-inclusiveness [in applying the hadiths containing threats] is present, even though the aforementioned opposing factor is not fit for opposition because the extent of it is for it to be said, "Construing it to apply to [both] cases of agreement *and* disagreement necessitates that some of those who are not deserving of the curse be included." So, it is said, "If the specification (*takhsis*) is contrary to the origin (i.e. the original indication of the general phrase), then its numerous occurrence is [also] contrary to the origin." So, excluded from this generalisation is he who is excused because of ignorance, *ijtihad*, or *taqlid* (i.e. following the judgment of a *mujtahid*), in spite of the fact that the ruling embraces those who are not excused. In addition, it embraces the cases where there is agreement (*suwar al-wifaq*). For surely specification occurs less [often]. So it (i.e. specification in this place) would be more fitting.

The Eighth [way of responding]: is to say that if we construe the expression to mean this, it would include mentioning the cause for the cursing. And the exception would remain while having the ruling lagging behind due to something that bars (*mani'*). And there is no doubt that he who promises or threatens is not obliged to exclude [mention of] the one in whose regard the promise or threat lags behind, due to something in opposition. As a result, the words would happen to be running on the path of correctness.

As for when we make the [attachment of] the curse apply to doing what has been unanimously considered to be forbidden, or if we make the cause for the curse [apply to] the belief [that is] in opposition to the consensus, the cause for the cursing would not be mentioned in the hadith, in spite of the fact that that generalisation also necessarily requires specification. So, if there must be specification under both presumptions, then its necessary application (*iltizam*) to the first is more fitting (i.e. the case of doing what is unanimously considered to be forbidden), because it conforms to the context (*wajh*) of the statement and [it] lacks in anything unspoken (*idmar*).

The Ninth [way of responding]: would be to say that what leads to this (*al-mujib li hadha*) is nothing more than the negation of the curse including the one who has an excuse (*ma'dhur*). And we have presented in what has passed that [with] the hadiths containing threats, the only thing meant by them is to clarify that that action [mentioned] is a reason for that curse. So, the presumption would happen to be that this action is the reason for the curse. Then, if this happens to be said, it does not result necessarily that the ruling applies with reference to every person. However, it does result necessarily that the reason is present whenever the ruling does not follow it. And there is nothing dangerous about that. We have determined in what has passed that blame does not attach to the *mujtahid* to the point that we say that the one who permits the forbidden is graver in sin than its doer. Despite this, the one with a [valid] excuse is pardoned. So, if it happens to be said, "So, who is punished? For surely the doer of this forbidden act is either a *mujtahid* or one who emulates one (*muqallid*), and both of them escape the punishment," [If they say this] we would say, "the answer is of different forms:

One of them: is that the intent is to clarify that this act necessitates punishment, whether one who does it is found or is not found. So, once it is presumed that there is no doer [of the act], while the condition for the punishment is removed in his regard or there exists what prevents it (i.e. the punishment), this does not damage its being forbidden. Rather, we know that it is forbidden, so that those who ascertain its impermissibility can avoid it. And it would be out of Allah's mercy to the one who does it that an excuse exists for him. And this is similar to how minor sins are forbidden even though they happen to be expiated by avoiding major sins. And this is the case of all forbidden acts over which there is disagreement [about their impermissibility]. So, if it comes to light that they are forbidden—even though the one who does them as a *mujtahid* or *muqallid* might happen to be excused, that does not keep us from believing them to be forbidden.

The Second: is to clarify that the ruling is a reason for removing the specious argument (*shubhah*) barring the attachment of the threat [to the doer]. For surely the excuse existing with the belief [in the act's permissibility] is not meant to remain. Rather, the aim is its removal to the extent possible (i.e. the removal of the belief in its permissibility). And if not for this, it would not be necessary to clarify the information (*'ilm*). And to leave people in their ignorance would be better for them. And to abandon the proofs of the problematic (*mushtabihah*) matters would be better than explaining them.

The Third: is that explaining the ruling and the threat is a cause for the one who avoids [sin] to remain firm in his avoidance. And if not for that, acting upon them would be widespread.

The Forth: is that this excuse would not be an excuse if one is incapable of removing it. Otherwise, whenever it is possible for the human being to know the truth and is thereafter negligent about it, such will not be pardoned.

The Fifth: is that there may happen to be amongst the people those who do the act without employing an *ijtihad* that would allow it and not following another's *ijtihad* (*muqallidan*) that would allow it. So, [with] this type [of person], the reason for the threat exists with him without this specific element that bars [him from punishment or blame]. So, he is exposed to the threat and it attaches to him unless another inhibitor exists with him, like repentance (*tawbah*), good deeds that erase [bad deeds], or other than that.

Additionally, this individual is in disarray (*mudtarib*). A person may think that his *ijtihad* or *taqlid* is permissible for him to do, and he may happen to be correct in that *at times* and in error at others. However, whenever he pursues the truth and [when] following lust does not dissuade him, then Allah does not burden a soul beyond its capacity.

The Tenth [way of responding]: is [to say] that if leaving these hadiths running to their demands necessitated that some *mujtahids* fall under the threat, then in the same way, to apply them outside of their demands would necessitate that some *mujtahids* fall under the threat. So, if *it* was a necessary result (*lazim*) in both cases presumed, the hadith would remain free of anything in opposition. So, it would be a duty to act upon it.

To clarify that is [to say] that many of the Imams have expressly stated that the one who does the act (*surah*) that is differed over [regarding its permissibility] is cursed. Among them are 'Abd Allah b. 'Umar ﷺ. For surely he was asked about the one who marries her (i.e. a woman) in order to make her permissible [to her first husband who divorced her three irrevocable divorces] while neither the woman nor her husband has any knowledge of that. He said:

> This is illicit intercourse (*safah*), not marriage. May Allah curse the one who made [her] permissible (*muhallil*) and the one [she was] made permissible for (*muhallal lahu*).

And this is recorded from him from more than one channel as well as from others (i.e. other scholars). One of them is Imam Ahmad b. Hanbal—may Allah show him mercy. For verily he said, "If he seeks to make [her] permissible (*ihlal*), then he is a *muhallil*, and he is cursed." And this is conveyed from groups of the Imams in many cases of disagreement in the topic of wine, interest, and others.

So, if the curse stated in scripture (*la'nah shar'iyah*)—and other things, like the threats that have come—only dealt with matters of agreement, then those [cursing] have cursed those who are not permitted to be cursed. Consequently, they are worthy of the threat that has come in more than one hadith, like his statement, "Cursing the Muslim is like killing him."[132] Also [like] his statement in what Ibn Mas'ud related ﷺ, "Reviling the Muslim is open defiance (*fusuq*). And fighting him is unbelief (*kufr*)." Agreed upon [by Bukhari and Muslim].

And Abu Al-Darda ﷺ heard Allah's messenger ﷺ say,

Verily the Disparagers (ta'anin) and the Cursers (la'anin) will be on the Day of Resurrection neither intercessors nor witnesses.

And on the authority of Abu Hurayrah ﷺ Allah's messenger ﷺ said, "It is not proper for a truly sincere person (*siddiq*) to be one who curses (*la'an*)." Muslim reported it.

And 'Abd Allah ibn Mas'ud ﷺ reportedly said, "Allah's messenger ﷺ said: "The believer is not the disparager, not the curser, and not the obscene (*fahish*), and not the foul-mouthed (*badhi*)." Tirmidhi reported it and said, "A fair hadith (*hasan*)."[133]

And in another Successor report (*athar*),[134] "There is not a single man who curses anything that does not deserve it, except that the curse returns to him."[135]

So, this threat that has come about cursing [another] to the point that it has been said that whoever curses one who does not deserve it, then that [individual] is the accursed one (*mal'un*). And indeed this curse is open defiance. And indeed it expels one from the status of *Siddiq* (*siddiqiyyah*), intercessor, and from being a witness [on the Day of Resurrection]. And it includes whoever curses one who does not deserve it.

So, if the one who does something over which there is disagreement does not fall under [the ruling of] the text, he is not deserving [of the curse]. As a result, his curser would be deserving of this threat. So, those *mujtahids* who held the view that the areas of disagreement enter into the hadith would be deserving of this threat.

Then, if the danger happens to be confirmed—while presuming that the areas of disagreement do not enter, and [also] while presuming they remain, it is known that it is not dangerous [to attach the curse], and that there is no objection in seeking evidence through the hadith [for the attachment of the curse].

And if the danger happens *not* to be confirmed—according

to one of the two presumptions (either that the curse refers to matters of disagreement or it does not), then there is definitely no danger that results necessarily [under either presumption].

And that is because when the inseparableness [between the all-inclusiveness of the phrase and them falling within its meaning] is established and it is known that for them to enter [within the meaning of the text] while presuming the existence [of danger] obliges that they enter while presuming the absence [of the same danger], then, what is confirmed is [either] one of the two matters, either the existence of the thing obligated (i.e. that they all enter) and the thing obligating (i.e. the all-inclusiveness of the phrase)—which is that they all enter. Or, the absence of the thing obligating and the thing obligated [is confirmed]—and it is that none of them enter [within the meaning], because when the thing obligated is found, the thing obligating is found. And when the thing obligating is absent, the thing obligated is absent.

And this measure is sufficient to invalidate the question. However, what we believe is that in reality (*waqi'*) they (the *mujtahid* and *muqallid*) do not enter according to both presumptions based on what has been determined. That is because entering under the threat is premised upon lacking an excuse in doing the act. As for the one who has a legally valid excuse, then the threat does not deal with him at all. And the *mujtahid* is pardoned. Rather, he is rewarded. So, the condition for entering [within the meaning of the text] is negated in his regard. So, he does not enter whether he happens to believe the hadith remains according to its apparent meaning or that there is a disagreement about that by which he is pardoned. And this is an argument that silences (*ilzam mufhim*). There is no option but to face one direction (*wajh wahid*). It is for the questioner to say, "I submit that there are among the *mujtahid* scholars those who believe that points of disagreement enter into the text relating to threats, and they threaten [others] in the areas of disagreement based upon this belief." So, he curses, for instance, the one who does that act. However, he errs in this belief a type of error wherein he is forgiven and rewarded. So, he does not enter into the threat of those who curse without right, because that threat, in my view, is construed according to a curse that is forbidden by consensus (*ittifaq*). So, whoever issues a curse forbidden by consensus exposes himself to the aforementioned threat about cursing. And when the curse is one of the topics of disagreement (*mawarid al-khilaf*), it does not enter into the hadiths about the threat, just as the deed wherein there is disagreement about its permissibility and cursing the one who does it does not enter into the hadiths about the threat.

So, just as you have excluded matters of disagreement from the first threat [about particular sins], he excluded matters of disagreement from the second threat [about cursing those who do not deserve it]. And he believed that the hadiths containing threats on both ends do not include matters of disagreement surrounding the permissibility of the act or the permissibility of cursing the one who does the act whether he believes the permissibility of the act or its impermissibility.

For I surely do not, according to both presumptions, deem it permitted to curse the one doing the act, and I do not permit cursing the one who curses the one doing the act. And I do not believe that the doer or the curser falls under the hadith of the threat. And I do not show harshness against the curser to the extent that those do who consider him as being subjected to the threat. Rather, cursing him is undoubtedly one of the matters of disagreement in my view, and particularly from the sum of matters related to *ijtihad*. But I believe him to be in error in that regard, just as I believe the one who permits it to be in error. For the positions concerning points of disagreement are three:

One of them: is the view of prohibition (i.e. one should give more strength to the side making the act prohibited)

The second: is the view of prohibition as well as the attachment of the threat [to the doer].

And the third: is the view of the impermissibility free of this severe threat.

And I might prefer this third view due to the existence of evidence that the deed is prohibited and that it is prohibited to curse the doer of the act over which there is disagreement [about its permissibility], in spite of my belief that this hadith mentioned about the threat of the doer and the threat of the curser does not include these two examples.

So, it is to be said to the questioner, "If you deem it possible that cursing this doer falls under matters of *ijtihad*, it is permissible to seek proof for it (i.e. the curse) through the apparent indication suggested (*zahir mansus*)." For surely, in this instance, one is not safe from having matters of disagreement included in the hadith of the threat when the thing that obligates them being included is present. So, it must be acted upon. And if you have not deemed it possible for it to be one of the matters of *ijtihad*, then cursing would be unequivocally prohibited. And there is no doubt that whoever curses a *mujtahid* a curse that is unequivocally prohibited, he falls under the threat mentioned about the curser—even if he happens to make a mistaken judgment (*muta'awwilan*), like those who curse some of the Pious Forbears (*Salaf Salih*).

So, it has been established that circular logic (*dawr*) is a necessary result (*lazim*), whether you decisively declare the prohibition against cursing the one who does that over which there is disagreement or if you tolerate the difference of opinion about it. And that belief that you mentioned does not prevent [anyone from] seeking proof through the texts containing threats in either of the two presumptions. And this is apparent.

It is also said to him, "Our aim from this example (*wajh*) is not to prove that the threat covers areas of disagreement. The aim is merely to prove the valid use of the hadith containing the threat as proof in areas of disagreement. In addition, the hadith indicates two rulings: the prohibition [of the act], and the threat [of punishment for doing it], while what you have mentioned merely deals with negating that it indicates the threat [of punishment]."

The aim here is merely to clarify how it indicates prohibition. So, once you have obliged yourself [to accept] that the hadiths that threaten the curser do not cover a curse wherein there is disagreement, there does not remain in the curse over which there is disagreement any evidence of its prohibition. And what we are involved in [discussing] of the curse is differed about as has preceded. So if it is not forbidden, it is permissible. Or it is said [to such a person], "So, if no evidence of its prohibition exists, it is not permissible to believe in its prohibition while the element necessitating its permissibility is present. It (i.e. the element) is the hadiths that curse the one who does this." And the scholars have differed about the permissibility of cursing such [a person], while there is no evidence of the prohibition against cursing him according to this presumption. So, it is a duty to act upon the evidence that necessitates the permissibility of cursing him, which is free of any opposition. And this invalidates the question.

Then, the matter has circled against the questioner from another regard. And this other circling has only occurred because most of the texts that forbid cursing include the threat. So, if it is not permitted to seek the texts containing threats as evidence for the areas of disagreement, it is not permitted that they be sought as proof for a curse over which there is disagreement as has preceded. And if one said, "I seek as evidence of the prohibition of this curse by consensus (*ijma'*)," it is said to him, "Consensus is held regarding the prohibition of cursing someone specific among the People of Virtue." As for cursing the one described, you already know the difference of opinion about it. And it has preceded that cursing the one described does not necessarily mean that it applies to every one of its particulars unless [all] the prerequisites are found and the inhibitors are removed. But the matter is not so.

It is also said to him, "All of what has preceded of evidence that point to the inadmissibility of construing these hadiths to apply to areas of agreement is rejected here." And they (i.e. the hadiths of threats) invalidate this question here, just as they invalidated the foundational question (*asl al-su'al*). And this does not fall under the category of '*making a proof one of the introductions to another proof*' so that it can be said, "This—in spite of being extensive—is only one proof."

[That is] because, the aim from it is to clarify that the danger they thought of is a necessary result according to [both] the presumptions. Consequently, it would not be a danger. So, one proof would happen to have indicated that areas of disagreement are intended from the texts, and that [they also indicated that] there is no danger in that. And it is not objectionable for a proof of a thing sought after to be an introduction for the proof of another thing sought after even if both things sought were inseparable.

The Eleventh [way of responding]: is to say that the scholars agree about the obligation of acting upon the hadiths containing threats in what they necessitate of prohibition. And some of them differed only about acting upon [all] their particulars (*ahadiha*) specifically regarding the threat.

So, as for [acting upon them] in the prohibition, there is no accounted for or considered disagreement. And the scholars among the Companions, Successors, and the jurists after them in their public addresses and their books never ceased to present them as proofs in the areas of disagreement and other [areas]. Rather, if there was a threat in the hadith, that was more eloquent in necessitating prohibition according to what all hearts acknowledge. The alert has also already preceded to [there being] greater weight given to the view of those who act upon them with respect to the ruling and in believing the threat, and that it is the view of the overwhelming majority. On this basis, no question that contravenes what the majority (*Jama'ah*) has agreed upon will be accepted.

The Twelfth [way of responding]: is to say that the texts containing threats from the Kitab and the Sunnah are many. And the adoption of what they necessitate is compulsory generally (*'ala wajh al-'umum*) and absolutely (*al-itlaq*) without any particular individual being specified whereas it cannot be said, "This individual is cursed, subjected to wrath, or deserving the Fire—especially if that person happens to have virtuous and good characteristics." For verily [with] everyone other than the Prophets it is possible for them [to commit] minor and major sins along with the possibility of that person being a *siddiq*, martyr, or righteous person (*salih*). This is due to what has preceded in that the thing necessitating the sin is removed from him by repentance, asking forgiveness, good deeds that erase [bad deeds], [patiently enduring] tribulations that expiate [sins], intercession [of the Prophet ﷺ], or the sheer will of Allah and His mercy. So, once we adopt what His statement necessitates, *Verily those who devour the wealth of orphans wrongfully, devours in their bellies no more than a fire. And they shall enter a blazing flame.* [Nisa: 10] or [we adopt what is necessitated by] His statement ﷻ, *And whoever disobeys Allah and His messenger and transgresses His limits, He will enter him into a Fire dwelling forever therein. And he shall have a humiliating chastisement.* [Nisa: 14] or [when we adopt what is necessitated by] His statement ﷻ, *O you who believe! Do not devour your wealth between you falsely unless it be a commerce by mutual satisfaction from you. And do not kill yourselves. Verily Allah is always merciful to you. And whoever does that from hostility and wrongfully, We will enter him into a Fire. And that is easy for Allah.* [Nisa: 29 – 30] and [add to that] other verses containing threats; Or [once] we adopt what his statement necessitates ﷻ, "May Allah curse he who drinks wine"[136] or "...is disrespectful to his parents" or "...changes the way-mark (*manar*) of the Earth[137]" Or, "May Allah curse the thief." [138] Or, "May Allah curse the devourer of usury, the one who gives it to devour, the two witnesses of it, and the one who records it."[139] Or, "May Allah curse the withholder of charity and the one who transgresses in it."[140] Or, "Whoever introduces a new thing in Medina or grants shelter to an innovator, then on him is the curse of Allah, the angels, and all of humanity."[141] Or, "Whoever drags his waistcloth out of conceit, Allah will not look at him on the Day of Resurrection."[142] Or, "Whoever has an ant's weight of pride in his heart will not enter Paradise."[143] Or, "Whoever defrauds us is not from us."[144] Or, "Whoever makes a claim to other than his father or claims clientage to other than his patrons, then Paradise is forbidden for him."[145] Or, "Whoever swears a false oath in order to take a portion of wealth of a Muslim man, he will meet Allah while He is angry at him."[146] Or, "Whoever makes the wealth of a Muslim man permissible with a false oath, Allah has made the Fire obligatory for him. And He has made Paradise forbidden for him."[147] Or, "The one who severs ties with the womb will not enter Paradise."[148] And include hadiths containing threats other than that. [Once we adopt what they necessitate] it is not permissible to specify a particular individual of those who do one of these actions. And we say, "[With] this specific individual, this threat is *not* applied to him as a result of the possibility of repentance and other things that eliminate the punishment."

[And once we adopt this] it is not permissible to say, "This necessitates cursing Muslims, cursing the Ummah of Muhammad ﷺ or cursing the *Siddiqin*, or the *Salihin*, since it is said: "The *Siddiq* and the *Salih*, when any of these acts issue from one of them, there must be an inhibitor that prevents attaching the threat to him in addition to the reason for it (i.e. the threat)."

So, the execution of these matters by those who think them to be permissible as a result of *ijtihad*, *taqlid*, or the like of that, the extent of it is that he happens to be one of the types of *siddiqs* from whom attaching the threat to is inadmissible due to something that bars; Just as attaching the threat to them is inadmissible because of repentance, good deeds that erase, or other reasons. And know that this path must be followed. For surely other than it are two evil roads.

One of them: is the view that attaches the threat to every individual by himself, while claiming that this is acting in accordance with the texts. This is more disgusting than the view of the Khawarij who accuse of unbelief for committing sin, as well as the Mu'tazilah, and others. And its invalidity is known by necessity from the religion of Islam. And its proofs are known in a place other than this one.

The second: is the abandonment of speaking and acting in accord with the hadiths of Allah's messenger ﷺ while thinking that speaking in accord with what it obliges necessitates condemning the one who acts in opposition to them.

This abandonment leads to misguidance and becoming included with the People of the [other] two scriptures who took their scholars (*ahbar*) and monks (*ruhban*) as lords instead of Allah as well as the Messiah, son of Mary. For surely the Prophet ﷺ said:

> *They did not worship them [literally]. Yet, they made lawful for them the unlawful, and then they followed them. And they made unlawful for them the lawful, and then they followed them.*[149]

And it leads to obedience to the creation in disobedience to the Creator. And it leads to an ugly end, and the misinterpretation understood from the gist of His statement ﷻ, *Obey Allah and obey the Messenger and those possessing command among you. Then if you dispute with one another in a thing, refer it to Allah and the Messenger if you indeed believe in Allah and The Last Day. That is better and best in result* [Nisa: 59]. Then, the scholars differ much.

So, every report containing severe censure (*taghliz*), if one happens to act in opposition to it, abandons stating what it contains of censure, or abandons acting upon it altogether, the inherent danger from this individual is what is graver than being characterised by unbelief (*kufr*) and straying from the religion. And if the danger happening from this individual is not graver than those before him, then he is [definitely] not beneath them [in sin]. So, we must believe in the entire Book and follow all that has been revealed to us from our Lord. And [we must] not have faith in some of the book and reject some [of it]. Our hearts are not to find ease in following some of the Sunnah while being averse to accepting some of it according to [our personal] customs and fancies. For, surely this is a departure from the straight way to the way of those whose portion is wrath and those who are astray.

So, may Allah direct us to what He loves. May He be pleased with our words and deeds that are good. And may He benefit us and all Muslims with well being.

And may Allah bless Muhammad—Seal of all Prophets, as well as his family, and his Companions—the rightly guided, his wives—the Mothers of the Faithful, and those following them in goodness until the Day of Judgment.

Appendix

Why Did the Imams Differ?

By Abdullah bin Hamid Ali

This chapter aims at disproving the claim that the Salaf only relied upon sahih reports that fulfill the conditions stipulated by Sunni hadith scholars. The reason is that many Muslims have made it a point to severely criticise and condemn many of the great scholars of our tradition, their works, and even the common Muslim who may happen to quote or act upon a weak hadith. Those condemning believe that quoting a weak hadith is tantamount to lying on the Prophet even though that has never been an accepted position adopted by Muslim scholars. True! It is closer to being a lie than the truth, but even that depends on how weak the hadith may be and in what area it is being employed, as we will come to see.

Nothing greater affirms this statement of mine than the fact that hadith scholars have always made a distinction between a fabricated hadith (mawdu) and a weak hadith (da'if). Why make a distinction between the two if the narration of a weak hadith is equal to the narration of one that is spurious and false? Additionally, even if we were to compare the two forms of agreed upon acceptable hadith *sahih* and *hasan*, we would find that the latter contains characteristics that make it weaker than the former even though we do not declare it to be weak. Furthermore, the same relativity exists when we compare an indisputably authentic hadith (*mutawatir*) with one that is reasonably authentic *(sahih ahadi)*.

The point is that weakness and strength in terms of reports and narratives differ in degree. The majority of our Pious Forbearers took this into account often in their acceptance and rejection of different reports. So one cannot rightfully reject a scholar's statement simply because the hadith he reports may have some weakness in it, unless the weakness found is something that the scholar himself declared to be a valid basis for rejecting such a hadith. In that case, it would be a case of an oversight on that scholar's part that must be taken into consideration. Our hope is that by the end of this essay, these facts will be borne out.

Appendix Ch.1

"If the hadith is sahih, it is My Madhhab"

What is often times used as a proof that the Four Imams did not intend for the common Muslim to uncritically follow them (taqlid) without knowing their evidence is the fact that they are reported as saying things like, "If the hadith is *sahih*, then it is my madhhab," etc. For the opponents of *taqlid*, this fact serves as decisive proof for the impermissibility of uncritical imitation of a scholar, and the obligation of demanding evidence from them. However, one must understand a few things about these statements to grant them their proper contexts and interpretations:

A -These statements were not addressed to the common lay Muslim. They were addressed to scholars who were qualified to exercise their own independent judgment (*ijtihad*) about religious matters. The proof for this is that [1] most of the Imams deem it impermissible for one *mujtahid* to uncritically follow another *mujtahid's* ruling until he has completed his scholarly endeavour (*ijtihad*)[150] ; [2] hadith books were not readily available to the masses during that era and the common folk did not know which books could be relied on and which could not; and [3] even if the books were available and known, the common person did not have the qualifications to determine the soundness or weakness of any particular report as is the case today. Furthermore [4], they were not familiar with the nomenclature of hadith scholars. So 'sahih' to the common person meant no more than 'healthy or true,' while it had a much more specialised meaning to the learned in later years.[151]

B -Another thing we need to consider about having a layperson ask a scholar for textual evidence is that [1] there is no jurisprudence or law that can be extracted from the translation of any hadith, while countless mistranslations exist; and [2] even if the person knows Arabic, as a layman, he still does not possess the qualifications of being a *mufassir* or *sharih* (commentator or interpreter) of the hadith. So demanding that scholar to present textual evidence to him would be just another lesson in futility, since what sense would it make for the scholar to give him the evidence when he does not have the tools to interpret them and to give it due scrutiny?

Appendix Ch.2

The Authentic Sunna – Conditions for the sahih Report

Hadith scholars have stipulated four conditions for a hadith to be considered sahih:

1. That it have a connected chain from start to end
2. That its transmitters all have impeccable character and memories
3. That the report not be irregular in so much that it contradicts the reports of all other transmitters of the same report or the reports of more reliable transmitters
4. And that the hadith not contain any subtle weaknesses[152]

When these conditions are fulfilled, a hadith is declared to be 'sahih': sound, authentic, or rigorously authenticated. One of the most important of those conditions is 'the reliability of the transmitters.' A transmitter is considered reliable when two conditions are fulfilled:

1. He is not known to commit any enormities or the habitual commission of a minor sin.
2. The other condition is that the person must have an impecca-

ble memory, known by the fact that it has been verified that the transmitter almost never makes a mistake in narrating an account, and relates it in the same way with the same words each time he is asked.[153]

Innocence from major sin grants us confidence that the person's consciousness of God hinders him from speaking untruths about the Messenger and about other people. The impeccable character of his memory gives us confidence that the words of the Messenger have been transmitted to us with the greatest of accuracy. Even if it is not expressed exactly the way the Messenger stated them, we have relative certainty that the original intent of his words have been preserved.[154]

So when taking all of these factors into account, we can have almost complete certainty that a hadith is acceptable, sound, or authentic. I say "almost," since—contrary to popular understanding—a *sahih* hadith is not considered to be a source of information that produces definitive knowledge (*'ilm*) according to the majority of Islamic legal theorists. Rather, it merely produces near definitive or near factual knowledge (*zann*) unless it is a type of *sahih* hadith called '*mutawatir*,' which is the truly "authentic" hadith.[155]

The reason for this is that—in spite of the degree of confidence we can place in such transmitters—we are still not in a position to say that it is 'impossible' for one of those transmitters to lie, forget, or err. It is just that we believe that they 'most likely' did not lie, forget, or err, since they did not lie, forget, or err in normal occasions.

Appendix Ch.3

The Mutawatir hadith

A *mutawatir* hadith can be defined as 'a *sahih* hadith reported from concurrent channels to the point that 100% certainty is established that the report is factual.' The scholars of hadith define it as:

> "The report given by a group so large that reason and custom declare it impossible to be the result of a planned agreement upon a lie, transmitted from a group of a like number, and remaining that way throughout the chain from beginning to end."[156]

A prime example of something that is *mutawatir* or indisputably authentic in the way they are reported are the verses and chapters of the Quran and the manner they were transmitted from generation to generation. So many have related it in each age to the point that we have no doubt that the Quran we have today is the same Quran revealed to the Messenger . To deny the Quran or any of its verses would be tantamount to apostasy.

Appendix Ch.4

The Four Imams & the Authentic Sunna

As stated before, a *sahih* hadith that is not *mutawatir* (indisputably authentic) does not produce 100% certainty that the account or report is factual, even though it produces near certainty of that. However, what does one do when another source of Islamic law and practice conflicts with the indications of a non-*mutawatir* *sahih* hadith? Does that source produce any certainty? Or is it instantly cancelled out as proof of anything? And if it does produce certainty, can or does it produce more certainty than the non-*mutawatir* hadith to the point that we can legitimately abandon the hadith altogether?

These were the questions that were pertinent to the Imams, and these same questions are the most pertinent to us in understanding how it was possible for one of our Imams not to act on a non-*mutawatir sahih* hadith. In what follows is a presentation of cases where some of the Imams preferred particular sources of *fiqh* to *sahih* hadith's.

I. When A Source of Law is Stronger Than a Sahih Hadith
A. MALIK IBN ANAS & THE ACTIONS OF THE SCHOLARS OF MEDINA — 179 AH

Due to the fact that a *non-mutawatir sahih* hadith does not produce complete certainty, whenever a report would contradict the 'Actions of the Scholars of Medina', Imam Malik would prefer their commonly acknowledged practice to the hadith even if it was *sahih* as long as it was not *mutawatir* (indisputably authentic). This is because he believed their agreement to produce greater certainty than a reasonably authentic report (*āhādī* hadith).

[1] For instance, there is a hadith stating that the Messenger of Allah said:

> "Let not one of you fast on the day of Jumu'a unless one fasts [one day] before it or fasts [one day] after it [too]."[157]

The majority of scholars used this hadith and others as basis for disapproving of anyone fasting specifically on Friday.[158] Malik, on the other hand, said when asked about it:

> "I have not heard anyone of the people of knowledge and jurisprudence or anyone of those who are emulated forbidding the fast of the day of Jumu'a, and to fast it is good."[159]

So he considered it to be a good day to fast in spite of the hadith reports on the matter.[160]

[2] A second example is Imam Malik's preference to uphold the Medinite custom of not reciting the *basmala* before *Al-Fatiha* or the following *sura* in Salat[161], in spite of the existence of the following hadith on the authority of Umm Salama who said:

> "The Messenger of Allah used to recite 'Bismil-

Appendix

lahir-Rahmanir-Rahim Al-Hamdu lillahi Rabbi l-'Alamin.'"

In spite of the existence of this hadith and others like it, Ibn Al-Qasim reports Imam Malik as saying:

"*Bismillahir-Rahmanir-Rahim is not to be recited in Salat in the compulsory prayer equally if [one is reciting] inaudibly to himself or audibly.*" He (Ibn Al-Qasim) said: Malik said: "*It is the Sunna [of Medina], and upon it I have reached the people [maintaining this practice].*" He (Ibn Al-Qasim) said: Malik said about reciting Bismillahir-Rahmanir-Rahim in the obligatory prayer: "*The situation (sha'n) [that prevails in Medina] is the abandonment of the recitation of Bismillahir-Rahmanir-Rahim in the obligatory prayer.*" He (Malik) said: "*No one is to recite [it] inaudibly or audibly, neither an Imam nor a non-Imam.*" He (Malik) said: "*But in the voluntary prayer (nafila), if one likes, he may do so,[162] and if he likes, he may abandon [it]. [All of] that is permitted (wasi').*" He (Ibn Al-Qasim) said: Malik said: "*A man is not to recite the ta'awwudh[163] during the compulsory prayer before the recitation [of Al-Fatiha]. But he recites the ta'awwudh in the standing of Ramadan (Tarawih) when he recites.*" He (Malik) said: "*Those who recite [during Ramadan] have remained constant upon reciting the ta'awwudh in Ramadan [from the earliest days] when they stand [for prayer]...*"[164]

[3] Another example of Malik giving preference to the normative religious customs of the Medinite scholars is his decision to not act on the hadiths that make mention of the Prophet ﷺ end-

ing the prayer with two *taslīms*. One of those hadiths is the one found in *Muslim* wherein 'Amir, the son of Sa'd ibn Abi Waqqas, said that his father said:

> "I used to see Allah's messenger give salām to his right and to his left to the extent that I could see the whiteness of his cheek."[165]

Shaykh Ahmed b. Muhammad b. Al-Siddiq relates in his *Masalik Al-Dilala Fi Sharh Masa'il Al- Risala* the following statement of Ibn 'Abd Al-Barr:

> "It has been related from flawed channels (ma'lūla) that are not sound (la tasihhu) that the Prophet ﷺ used to offer one taslīm. However, it has been related that the Four Khulafā, Ibn 'Umar, Anas, Ibn Abi Awfa, and a group of the Successors (Tabi'in) used to offer one taslīm. But conflict exists about [the reports of] most of them whereas it has been related that they offered two taslīms just as it has been related that they offered one taslim. But the widespread well-known practice in Medina was in accord with it (one taslīna)..."

This last statement that "But the widespread well-known practice in Medina was in accord with it" is the clearest proof that the practice of the scholars of Medina was to end the prayer with only one *taslim*, not two. For this reason Imam Malik did not act upon the hadiths that mention two *taslīms*, while every narration of one *taslim* according to the scholars is weak[166] negating any attempt of Malik using them as a basis to substantiate his position.

Malik said:

> "On the authority of Nafi', Ibn 'Umar[167] used to give

salām to his right, and then he would reply to the Imam."

Ibn Al-Qasim said:

"*Malik adheres to it today. Malik said: "Then if there is someone on his left, he replies to him [too].""*[168]

Ibn Al-Qasim also said:

"*The Prophet ﷺ gave salam once as did Abu Bakr, 'Umar, 'Uthman, 'Umar b. 'Abd Al-'Aziz, 'A'isha*[169], *Abu Wa'il—i.e. Shaqiq, Abu Raja' Al-'Ataridi, and Al-Hasan [Al-Basri].*"[170]

[4] The last example I would like to give of Imam Malik forsaking the *sahih* hadith for the normative practice of the scholars of Medina is the matter of his decision not to act on the reports that make mention of the Prophet ﷺ raising his hands during each movement of the Salat. Imam Bukhari reports the following narration on the authority of Salim ibn 'Abd Allah b. 'Umar who reports from his father that:

"*The messenger of Allah used to raise his hands parallel with his shoulders when he started the Salat and when he said the takbīr for rukū' (bowing). When he raised his head from rukū', he raised them also in the same manner and said: "Sami' Allahu liman 'amidahu, Rabbanā wa laka al-'amd." But he did not do that while prostrating (sujud).*"

Malik said:

"*I do not know of raising the hands in any of the tak-*

bīrs of Salat, not in any lowering or any rising, except for at the start of the Salat. One raises his hands lightly. The woman in that [matter] is like the man [so she does likewise]."

Ibn Al-Qasim said:

"Raising the hands was weak in the view of Malik except for in the opening takbīr (takbiratu l-ihram)."[171]

B. ABU HANIFA & HANAFIS — 150 AH

Abu Hanifa, like Malik, had principles and sources of law and practice that he considered to be avenues that lead to greater certainty than *non-mutawatir* hadiths. An example of this is that if a particular Companion relating a hadith was not known as one of those who were foremost in learning, and the report conflicted with the proper judgment of legal analogy (*qiyās*), 'Hanafis[172] would consider legal analogy to be stronger than a *non-mutawatir* hadith. Consequently, they would abandon the hadith for legal analogy.

[1] For example, Abu Hurayra, one of the most well-known Companions who was not considered among their scholars in spite of relating a number of hadiths, once related the hadith that states the Prophet ﷺ as saying:

"Make wudu (ablution) from whatever fire has touched."[173]

When the Companion, 'Abd Allah b. 'Abbas, one of the most learned Companions, heard Abu Hurayra relate this hadith, Ibn 'Abbas said:

"And what if you happen to make wudu with heated water? Would you make wudu from it too?"

Abu Hurayra remained silent as if dumbfounded by this proposition.[174]

This example was sufficient for Hanafis to establish a precedent for the rule that 'When a transmitter not known to be a scholar (in spite of being righteous) gives a report that contradicts legal analogy, legal analogy is preferred to it.'

Another example of this is that Abu Hurayra reports that the Prophet ﷺ said:

> "Do not leave the teats of camels and small livestock full of milk. If so, the one who purchases it after that has the better of two options after he milks it. If he is pleased with it, he may retain it. If he dislikes it, he may return it along with it a saa'[175] of dried dates."

In other words, he may return it along with it a *saa'* of dried dates in place of milk. The demands of legal analogy are that if someone destroys the property of another, an equivalent form of that property must be insured if an equivalent exists. If not, the value of that item must be refunded. However, this hadith stipulates that—in spite of there being an equivalent item present—it may be replaced with something that it is not equivalent to it. Early Hanafis ruled that the judgment of legal analogy should be followed in this case, because Abu Hurayrah was not one of the learned Companions. He was simply a hadith transmitter. Since most hadiths are transmitted by meaning, there is the fear that the unlearned Companion may have improperly understood the words of the Messenger before conveying to others what he understood from the Prophet ﷺ.

Based on this rationale, the dictates of legal analogy produces greater certainty than the actual report does. So in such cases, the report is abandoned for what produces greater certainty.[176]

Hanafis also stipulate that in order to accept a non-*mutawatir* hadith it cannot conflict with the Quran or what is called the Sunna *Mashhura* (Popular Sunna).

1. CONTRADICTION WITH THE QURAN

- Imam Malik reports in his *Muwatta* that the Prophet ﷺ said: "Whoever touches his penis let him make *wudu*." In Imam Abu Hanifa's view, this hadith contradicts the Quran. For Allah says in [9: 108] "...*In it (the mosque) are men who love to become cleansed...*" This verse was revealed with regard to a group of men from the Ansar who chose to clean themselves with stones and water together after urinating. Touching one's genitals when cleansing one's self after answering a call of nature is inescapable. So if such a thing truly invalidated ablution (*wudu*), why would Allah praise men who do such a thing? Or, how could Allah refer to such men as being clean and pure after touching an unclean impure member of the body? If touching the genitals rendered a person impure, then Allah would not have praised these men for doing an impure act. In addition, the fact that the ablution was made compulsory by virtue of urination has no effect on this line of reasoning, because praise was given in spite of them doing the unavoidable act of touching their genitals. So the genitals are a clean part of the body. Consequently, the one who touches it is not required to renew his ablution.

- The Prophet ﷺ said, "There is no marriage without a guardian." He also said, "Any woman who marries off herself without the permission of her guardian, then her marriage is invalid, invalid, invalid!" In the view of Abu Hanifa, this hadith contradicts Allah's saying of women, "...*So do not prevent them from marrying their husbands*" [2: 232]. Consequently, he considered the marriages of women of full adult age who married without their guardians' permission to be valid.

2. THE SUNNA MASHHURA (THE POPULAR SUNNA)

The '*sunna mashhura*' or 'the popular sunna' is defined as "The hadith related by a number of Companions whose number does not reach the point of making it *mutawatir*, but becomes *mutawatir* in every succeeding stage in the chain." Such a hadith is

100% confirmed on the authority of the particular Companion it is attributed to, while it is not indisputably authentic concerning what is ascribed to the Prophet ﷺ in it.[177]

Another reason Hanifis give for not acting on a non-*mutawatir* sahih hadith is that it might contradict a *sunna mashhura* report. If such a conflict were to occur, the non-*mutawatir sahih* hadith would be ignored.

An example of this is the hadith that states:

> "The Prophet ﷺ judged in favour of a person on the basis of one witness and an oath."

In the view of Abu Hanifa, this contradicts the *sunna mashhūra* report that states:

> "The burden of proof is on the claimant, and the oath is upon the one who denies."

3. MATTERS THAT ARE CONSIDERED A UNIVERSAL NEED

Abu Hanifa would also disregard non-*mutawatir sahih* hadiths if it was a matter considered to be a universal need. The argument behind this is that matters that are universal needs should necessarily be common knowledge that the Prophet ﷺ shared to more than just a few people. So if it happens that only a few people related the report, the Imam would not accept any claims of its authenticity. Examples of this follow.

- The Prophet ﷺ said, "Whoever touches his penis let him make *wudu*." We already stated that Abu Hanifa rejected this hadith, because he believed that it contracted the aforementioned Quranic verse. A second reason he gave for not accepting it was that the matter mentioned in the hadith was a universal need. So more than just a few narrators should have known it.

- Another example is the hadith, "The two parties of a transaction have a choice [to a refund] as long as they have not dispersed, unless it is a sale with the option [to refund]." Abu Hanifa's view was that since business transactions are universal needs and should be common knowledge, such rules may not be established by non-*mutawatir sahih* hadiths. Consequently, he considered transactions to be final once the exchange is completed, with no right to annulment even if the two parties are still in one another's company.[178]

C. AHMED B. HANBAL — 241 AH

As for Imam Ahmed, he held the view that nothing can be placed over a hadith of the Prophet ﷺ. He believed this so deeply that it has been accepted by scholars of his school that he preferred to employ a weak hadith before he took refuge to legal analogy (*qiyas*). Some claim that when Imam Ahmed says 'weak' (*da'if*) he actually means 'fair' (*hasan*). This is found although the term, *hasan*, had not yet been coined with its popularly distinct meaning until after the time of Imam Ahmed during whose time only two kinds of hadiths existed: *sahih* and *da'if*.[179] Surrendering to the validity of this explanation does not completely remove confusion from this matter, because it would still mean that he considered '*hasan*' to be weak (*da'if*).

D. MUHAMMAD B. IDRIS AL-SHAFI'I - 204 AH

As for Imam Shafi'i, he was very strict when it came to accepting hadiths. In addition, he argued that after the Quran, nothing should be placed over the hadiths of the Prophet ﷺ regardless of it is *mutawatir sahih* or non-*mutawatir sahih*.

This difference between his position and the position of Imam Ahmed was that Shafi'i accepted no weak hadiths except in very special circumstances unless it was verified as being strengthened by an auxiliary chain that was *sahih*.[180]

II. WHEN A HADITH IS NOT SAHIH

It has become commonplace to hear that 'The *minhaj* of the Salaf was to follow only *sahih* hadiths.' In fact, the Salaf had no uniform methodology when it came to acceptance and rejection of hadiths except for in certain areas. In this section, I plan to disprove this claim by presenting the views of the Imams of the Salaf: Abu Hanifa, Malik, Shafi'i, and Ahmed. In particular, I would like to focus on their views as relates to the 'incompletely transmitted hadith' or 'report with undisclosed intermediaries' termed '*mursal.*'

MURSAL HADITH

The technical definition of a *mursal* hadith is: "A Successor's (*Tabi'i*) claim that the Prophet ﷺ said, did, or approved of something whether the Successor is one who took most of his knowledge from the Companions or one who took most of his knowledge from other Successors."[181] The essential problem with a *mursal* hadith is that it does not disclose its sources. In other words, the Successor does not mention what Companion heard the Prophet ﷺ say or do the particular thing claimed, just as it does not disclose whether or not that particular Companion was the one who told him. This then opens the door to the possibility that one or more other Successors had actually informed the Successor. There is then a possibility that one or more of those Successors may be unreliable as narrators. In spite of this, three of the four Imams accepted *mursal* hadiths in areas of practice and for general encouragement toward good.[182] Those three Imams were: Abu Hanifa, Malik, and Ahmed.[183] As for Shafi'i,[184] he only accepted *mursal* hadiths if it came from a *Tabi'i* who took most of his knowledge of the Sunna from the Companions,[185] like Sa'id b. Musayyab,[186] as long as an auxiliary report with a connected chain corroborates the *Tabi'i's* report.[187]

III. WEAK REPORTS THAT ENCOURAGE VIRTUOUS ACTIONS AND MERITS

To add to this discussion about the approach of the Salaf regarding the hadiths, I would like to bring to light the fact that the overwhelming majority of scholars accepted and considered legitimate the narration of weak reports that encouraged good works and spoke of meritorious qualities.

Imam Nawawi states in the introduction to his Forty-hadith along with its commentary the following:

> "The scholars have agreed upon the permissibility of acting according to the weak hadith[188] with respect to the meritorious works."[189]

Shaykh al-Islam Ibn Taymiyya says:

> "It is not permitted to rely in the Shariah upon weak hadith's that are neither sahih nor hasan. However, Ahmed b. Hanbal and other scholars deemed it permissible to narrate in the subject of meritorious acts when it is not known to be established as long as it is not known to be a lie. That is because when it is known that an act has been legislated by a scriptural proof and a hadith has been reported regarding its merit while it is not known to be a lie it is possible for the reward of it to be true. And not one of the Imams has said that it is not permissible for a thing to be made compulsory or recommended by a weak hadith. Whoever says such a thing has contravened consensus (ijma')...So it is permissible to relate reports that encourage good and discourage wrong as long as it is not known to be a lie. However, that applies to what one knows that Allah has encouraged or discouraged through evidence other than such a hadith whose condition is unknown."[190]

Finally, Nawawi says:

> "And it is permissible according to the scholars of ha-

dith and others to abandon strictness regarding chains of narration and to relate any weak hadith other than what is spurious, and to act upon it without clarifying its weakness in all besides the attributes of Allah— Most High, the rulings of religious practice, like the lawful and unlawful and from what is unconnected with creed and legal rulings."[191]

CONCLUSION

In light of all these facts, let it be said no more that the *Minhaj* of the Salaf was to only accept *sahih* hadiths. Let it be known that any time the Imams spoke of abandoning opinions in acceptance of the reports from the Prophet ﷺ, he or they were only addressing their students who were equally qualified to exercise scholarly endeavour (*ijtihad*). These were not statements intended for the common Muslim, since such people did not and do not have the qualifications to make a judgment about the authenticity, weakness, or interpretation of the holy scripture and related texts. Allah orders us in the Quran, "Then, Ask the People of the Reminder if you do not know" [16: 43]. He said, "And if they had referred it to the Messenger and to those in command from them, those who do extract it would have known it" [4: 83]. What this establishes is that there are two types of people in terms of knowledge: [1] Those that are qualified to interpret the scripture; and [2] those that are not. Those who are not qualified to interpret the scripture are to refer back to those who can in all matters that neither the Quran nor Sunna gives a clear judgment in its regard. Referring it back to them does not mean to ask them for their evidence. It means to accept their judgment in the matter based on their knowledge of the evidence, qualification to make such a judgment, and their moral integrity that protects them from speaking out of turn. Were it to mean that every lay Muslim is to ask what the scholar's evidence is, it would then mean that permission is given to the unlearned to interpret the Holy Scripture in spite of the fact that he is unqualified to interpret it. When the qualified scholar (*mujtahid*) makes a judgment and is mistaken, he is forgiven but rewarded for his scholarly endeavour (*ijtihad*).[192] The same does not apply to the layperson. Rather, the lay person is in sin for interpreting the Holy Scripture for his lack of qualification to do so. For this reason, the Prophet ﷺ said, "Whoever explains the Quran by what he sees and hits the mark has missed it."[193] He severely scolded a group of people during his time who gave judgment by what they knew from the Quran and Sunna for a man who had a wound and later had a wet dream. They told him that he could not simply make *wudu* before praying. So he performed *ghusl* instead, and died as a result. When word got back to the Prophet ﷺ, he said of them:

> "They killed him! May Allah kill them! Do they not ask when they do not know? The only cure for ignorance is to ask."[194]

This narration, if it is valid to use as evidence, is a clear example of how a person may have some knowledge of the Sunna, but still not be qualified to make a judgment. It also clarifies that such a person is sinful for offering a legal opinion when he lacks qualification. But even if this hadith is not sound (*sahih*) or fair (*hasan*), the rules outlined in the Quran and other reports from the Sunna support this understanding.

May Allah bring us out the darkness into light again and again until we can witness the brilliance and splendour of His face.

Notes

1. Ibn al-Zamlakani (662-727 AH), Abu al-Ma'ali Muhammad b. Ali b. 'Abd Al-Wahid was an Ash'ari theologian and Shafi'i jurist. He was a direct descendant of the Ansari companion Abu Dajanah Samak b. Harb and the leading Shafi'i scholar of his time. He was born in Damascus during the second half of the 7thcentury AH and was a contemporary of Ibn Taymiyah (661-728 AH). Interestingly, he was born one year after and died one year before the latter. Ibn al-Zamlakani praised Ibn Taymiyah as a mujtahid, but also wrote in refutation of his views regarding the triple divorce and the visitation of the tombs of the Muslim saints.

2. Ibn Kathir, Abu al-Fida al-Dimashqi. Al-Bidayah wa al-Nihayah, Beirut: Maktabah al-Ma'arif, 1988, 14/137.

3. In the 1418/1997 version of *Majmu'at al-Fatawa* of Dar al-Jil publishing house of Riyadh, Saudi Arabia, the Book of Sufism (*Kitab al-Tasawwuf*) is the sixth of 19 volumes, which has two sections beginning with *Kitab al-Tasawwuf*, section 11. Ibn Taymiyah says in this book:

    > All praise is due to Allah. As for the word 'Sufism' (*Tasawwuf*), it was not popular during the three [virtuous] generations. But speaking about it did become popular after that [period]. And it has been transmitted from more than one of the Imams and Shaykhs, like Imam Ahmad b. Hanbal, Abu Sulayman Al-Darani, and others. It has been related that Sufyan Al-Thawri spoke of it. And some say the same about Hasan Al-Basri. They differed with one another about the meaning that is to be attached to the 'Sufi.' For verily it is one of the nouns of affinity (*asma an-nasab*), like Qurashi,

  Madani, and the likes of that… [p. 7]

To know the true stance of Imam Taymiyah about Sufism, read this volume in its entirety.

4. Abu Dawud and Tirmidhi reported it as well as Ibn Hibban in his *Sahih* on the authority of Ibn 'Abbas with the wording: "Verily a man cursed the wind in the presence of Allah's messenger ﷺ. So he said, "Do not curse the wind. For surely it is commanded [to do what it does]. Whoever curses something that doesn't deserve it, the curse returns to him."

5. Imam Ahmad and others reported it from the hadith of Qabisah b. Dhu'ayb while omitting the Companion (*mursal*). And it has other chains of narrations with Companions omitted (*mursal*).

6. Translator's note: This is a reference to Surah 24 *Al-Nur*, verses 27-29 wherein Allah says, *O you who believe! Do not enter houses other than your own houses until you ascertain welcome and greet their inhabitants. That is best for you; perhaps you will be reminded. And if you do not find anyone therein, do not enter them until permission has been given you. And if it is said to you, "Go back," then go back; it is purer for you. And Allah is Knowing of what you do. There is no blame upon you for entering houses not inhabited in which there is convenience for you. And Allah knows what you reveal and what you conceal.*" It is reported in Imam Bukhari's *Sahih* that Abu Musa Al-Ash'ari once visited 'Umar b. Al-Khattab and asked permission to enter three times, but permission was not given. So he left. Then 'Umar said: "Did I not hear the voice of 'Abd Allah b. Qays asking permission [to enter]? Let him in!" But when they searched for him, they found that he had already left. So when he came the next time, 'Umar said to him, "What made you leave?" He said, "I asked permission three times, and permission was not given for me. I heard the Prophet ﷺ say, "When one of you asks permission three times and permission is not given to him, let him depart." Then 'Umar said, "You will surely bring me clear proof of this (i.e. a witness that the Prophet said it). Otherwise, I will hurt you with a beating!" So he went to an assembly of the Ansar and mentioned to them what 'Umar said. Then they said, "None other than the youngest of us will testify for you." So Abu Sa'id Al-Khudri stood up and told 'Umar of that [statement]. Then

'Umar said, "Bargaining in the market places distracted me [from hearing that]."

7. Imam Ahmad and Tirmidhi reported it. And he (Tirmidhi) said, "*hadith hasan sahih.*"

8. [It is] a hadith with an omitted Companion intermediary (*mursal*). Shafi'i reported it in his *Musnad*, and Bukhari and others reported it by way of 'Umar that he did not take tribute from the Zoroastrians until 'Abd Al-Rahman b. 'Awf testified that Allah's messenger ﷺ took it from the Zoroastrians of Hajar (Translator = town in Bahrain).

9. [It is] a place near Sham between Al-Maghithah and Tabuk. And it was said: A place at a distance of 13 *marhalahs* (Translator = i.e. 13 days journey) from the Enlightened City (Translator = Medina).

10. Bukhari and Muslim reported it by way of 'Abd Al-Rahman b. 'Awf.

11. Muslim reported it by way of 'Abu Sa'id Al-Khudri. And Imam Ahmad, Tirmidhi, and Ibn Majah reported it by way of 'Abd Al-Rahman b. 'Awf. And its wording is: "When one of you doubts in his Salat and does not know if he has prayed one (T. = i.e. one rak'ah) or two, then let him make it one…"

12. Muslim reported in his *Sahih* on the authority of 'Aishah who said, "The Prophet used to say when the wind blew: "O Allah! Verily I ask from You its good, the good of what is in it, and the good of what is sent with it. And I take refuge with You from its evil, the evil of what is in it, and the evil of what is sent with it.'" And Abu Dawud, and Ibn Majah reported on the authority of Ibn 'Abbas who said, "I heard Allah's Messenger ﷺ say: "The wind is from Allah's spirit. It brings mercy. And it brings punishment. So when you see it, do not revile it. But ask Allah for its good, and seek refuge with Allah from its evil." Hafiz Ibn Hajar said, "The hadith is *hasan sahih.*"

13. Bukhari reported it on the authority of 'Abd Allah b. 'Abbas.

14. Bukhari and Muslim reported it form the hadith of 'Aishah.

15. Muslim reported it from the hadith of 'Ali. Ahmad, Abu Dawud, and Tirmidhi reported it from the hadith of Khuzaymah b. Thab-

it. Daraqutni related it. And Ibn Khuzaymah graded it as sound (*sahih*) from the hadith of Abu Bakrah Nufai' b. Al-Harith. And these hadiths clarify the interval of wiping the leather socks as one day and one night for the non-traveler and three days with their nights for the traveler. Tirmidhi said, "And it is the view of the people of knowledge from the Prophet's Companions, and the Successors (*Tabi'un*) after them among the jurists (*Fuqaha*).

16. Imam Ahmad reported it. And Timidhi graded it as sound from the hadith of Furay'ah t.

17. Translator: An authority figure should not accept gifts from people under him, because it can be construed as being an offering done to receive personal favours.

18. Imam Ahmad reported it in his *Musnad*.

19. Imam Ahmad and Tirmidhi reported that Abu Bakr heard the Prophet say, "There is not a single man who commits a sin, makes lustrations (*wudu*), does his lustrations well, prays two units (*rak'ahs*), and then asks Allah for forgiveness except that he is forgiven." Then he read this verse: *And those who when they commit an indecency or have wronged themselves, they remember Allah and then ask forgiveness for their sins…* [Surah Ali 'Imran 3: 135] And Ibn Hajar mentioned that the hadith's chain is *jayyid* [Translator: *Jayyid* translates as 'good.' A chain of transmission is called '*jayyid*' when a scholar has trouble determining if it should be classified under '*sahih*' (sound) or '*hasan*' (fair). Refer to Suyuti's comments in *Tadrib Al-Rawi* pp. 111-112]

20. Translator: This means that if the time of her pregnancy is more than 4 months and 10 days—the determined minimum period for mourning, she does not have to wait another 4 months and 10 days after she gives birth. But if the time left for the pregnancy is fewer than 4 months and 10 days, she has to add 4 months and 10 days to her waiting period after giving birth before she can remarry.

21. Bukhari and Muslim reported it on the authority of Subay'ah Al-Aslamiyyah.

22. Translator: A *shahid* (singular of *shawahid*) is the title given to a separate report that strengthens another due to it conveying a meaning similar to the report under consideration while not

being the same incident reported.

23. Translator: A *mutaba'a* (singular of *mutaba'at*) is the title given to a separate report that strengthens another by coming from a different chain of narration. In this case, the hadith is the same incident reported in the hadith under consideration.

24. This first view—that if the original transmitter does not recall relating the hadith, the hadith should not be accepted—is the view of Abu Hanifa, while the other view is held by the overwhelming majority. See *Miftah al-Wusul* of Tilmasani pp. 322-328.

25. Translator: This view has been transmitted by a number of the scholars of the early community in Medina. It has also been related from Shafi'i, Habib b. Thabit, Ibn Shihab al-Zuhri, Tawus, Hisham b. 'Urwah, Ibn al-Mubarak, and many others. See Suyuti's comments on this in *Tadrib al-Rawi* pp. 47-48.

26. Translator: Saying that the hadith is a proof regardless of where it originates does not translate to mean that Ibn Taimiyah considered the view of those who believed that it mattered where the hadith originated to be a matter of heresy or a sign of misguidance. Rather, it actually shows how he did give credence to those views, because by accepting hadiths regardless of their regional origin one accepts the credibility of those who do believe it matters where the hadith originates. Consequently, he accepts the validity of that *ijtihad*. He just believes that it is an improper stipulation to have for accepting a hadith, especially since he was an adherent of the Hanbali School of law.

27. Translator: Like Abu Hanifa, the Shi'a, and others. Refer to *Usul al-Shashi* pp. 280-283, and *SHIA* by Tabatabai p. 102 and *Bihar al-Anwar* 1/139. This does not mean that the other scholars from the Sunnis do not give consideration to whether or not the hadiths contradict with the Quran in order to authenticate them. It is just that there are a number of instances when this rule is utilised by Hanafis and Shiites and where they make the claim that there is a contradiction, the others dispute these claims and seek to reconcile the apparent contradictions.

28. Translator: This is the view of many Hanafis. They rejected the hadith that obligates *wudu* for eating food that has been touched

by fire as related by Abu Hurayrah but opposed by Ibn 'Abbas on the basis of legal analogy. This opinion is premised on the view that anytime a Companion who was not considered a scholar related a hadith that opposed the outward judgment of legal analogy (*qiyas*), then legal analogy is more authoritative. So the hadith should be abandoned, since it was customary for the Companions to relate reports from the Prophet ﷺ in their own words as they understood him e. So if the person is not one of the learned, there is the possibility that he misunderstood the intent of the Messenger ﷺ. So, legal analogy should be given precedence over his report. But, some Hanafis differed with this rule. See *Usul al-Shashi* pp. 275-279 and *Miftah al-Wusul* pp. 316-322.

29. Translator: This is another Hanafi principle that posits, "When something should be common knowledge due to it being of the highest importance, then more than just a few transmitters should have reported the statement." So when only one or a few report the hadith, the hadith is considered to be weak. And it needs to be reported by indisputable transmission (*tawatur*) before it can be acted on. For this reason, they do not accept the ruling that a man must perform *wudu* for touching his genitals, which has been transmitted from the Prophet e, as well as similar matters. See *Miftah al-Wusul* pp. 315-317. Also have a look at *Usul al-Shashi* pp. 284-286.

30. Translator: That is, he made dry ablution (*tayammum*) with dirt.

31. Bukhari and Muslim reported it. The authors of the *Sunan* collections also did so with similar wordings.

32. He reported it from Abu Ya'la, Daraqutni, and others. Refer to *Al-Bidayah wa al-Nihayah* of Ibn Kathir: [7/24].

    Translator: Hafiz Abu Ya'la reports on the authority of Abu Hazim Al-Mazani that he said, "I witnessed 'Ali and Zubayr when they faced one another [during the Battle of the Camel]. 'Ali said to him, "O Zubayr! I implore you by Allah! Did you not hear Allah's Messenger ﷺ say: 'Verily you will fight me and you will be wrong'?" He (Zubayr) said, "Yes." I did not remember it until I stood here in this place." So he left [the battlefield]." This is also reported by Bayhaqi and others with different wordings.

33. Translator: The Salaf is the name given to the first three generations or 300 years of Islam after the emigration from Mecca

to Medina. And the Khalaf is the name given to the righteous generations that came after the first three.

34. In *Al-Qamus*: "*Al-Muzabanah*: is the sale of plump ripe dates still on the date-palm tree for dry dates. And it is [the same meaning as the word] '*Al-Zabn*'. It means '*to push*' (*daf*). It is as if each one of the parties of the sale pushes his counterpart away from his right using what is added from his side. And it has been prohibited for not knowing [the exact measure or amount of what is being sold] and the price-fraud (*ghabn*) entailed."

35. *Al-Mukhabarah* (share-cropping): is to farm [land] for half [the yield] or the like of it. It has been said: It is [synonymous with the word] *Muzara'ah*.

36. *Al-Muhaqalah*: is the sale of wheat (*zar'*) before it is fit to consume, or selling them on an ear for *hintah* (wheat not on an ear). Or [it is] share-cropping (*muzara'a* done) for a third, a fourth, less, or more. Or it is to rent land for wheat. *Al-Hiqlah* is the clean water that remains in a pond. It takes all three vowels [on each letter of its root]. *Al-Haqlah* with *fathah* is a disease found in camels and a wound in the stomach of horses that results from eating dirt.

37. *Al-Mulamasah:* means touching *(al-mumassah)*. It is to say, "*Lamastu wajhi*" (I touched my face). And in business transactions it is to say, "*Idha lamastu thawbaka…*" (when I touch your garment) or "*Idha lamasta thawbi…*" (when you touch my garment) "*…the transaction is complete with such and such [price] (faqad wajaba al-bay'u bi kadha*). Or it is to touch the item from behind a garment without looking at it.

38. *Al-Munabadhah:* is to say, "*unbudh ilayya al-thawba*" (toss to me the garment), or "*anbudhuhu ilayka*" (I will toss it to you), "*…the transaction is complete with such and such or such and such [price].*" Or it is to throw the garment to him and for him to throw something similar to it. Or it is to say, "*Idha nabadhtu al-hasata wajaba al-bay'u*" (when I toss the stones the transaction is complete).

39. *Al-Gharar:* is what would dupe the buyer from its exterior while its interior is unknown.

On the authority of Abu Hurayra. He said, "Allah's Messenger

ﷺ forbade the sale by tossing stones (*bay'u al-hasat*), and the sale with [avoidable] risk (*bay'u al-gharar*)." Muslim reported it.

And on the authority of Anas. He said, "Allah's Messenger ﷺ forbade *muhaqalah, mukhadarah, mulamasah, munabadhah,* and *muzabanah.* Bukhari reported it.

And on the authority of Jabir the Prophet forbade *muhaqalah, muzabanah,* and *mukhabarah.* Abu Dawud and Nasa'i reported it. And Tirmidhi graded it as sound (*sahih*). And *mukhadarah* is the sale of fruit before they are fit to consume.

40. *Al-Ighlaq*: is coercion (*ikrah*). Abu 'Ubayda said, "*Al-Ighlaq*: is to make something narrow (*tadyiq*)." Ibn Al-Qayyim Al-Jawziyah said, "Our Shaykh said: "*Al-Ighlaq*: is the closing of the door to knowledge and to striving for it. So the divorce initiated by the one of weak intelligence (*ma'tuh*), the insane, the drunkard, and the angry man who does not comprehend what he is saying enters into it (its meaning), since each of these has closed over himself the door of knowledge and striving for it. And divorce only happens *via* one who intends it while having knowledge of it. And Allah knows best."

41. Imam Nawwawi states in *Sharh Muslim* (7/130 Chapter 5: *Kitab al-Ashriba*) in speaking about the reports forbidding *nabidh*, "Our view and the view of the overwhelming majority is that this prohibition is indicative of strong discouragement only (*karahat al-tanzih*) and that is not unlawful (*haram*) as long as it does not transform into an intoxicant. And the overwhelming majority of the scholars have taken this view. But some of the Malikis said: "It is unlawful (*haram*).""

42. Translator: It was the view of Abu Hanifah that only the wine made from grapes was impermissible for one to drink, since this is what the word '*khamr*' (mentioned in the Quran) means in its origin. For that reason, he allowed the drinking of wine made from wheat, barley, and the like, to the degree that they do not produce intoxication. But, the degree that produces intoxication is considered to be unlawful (*haram*). As for Malik, Shafi'i, and Ahmad, they considered all forms of intoxicants to be unlawful (*haram*) whether one drinks enough that produces intoxication or not. And one is punished for drinking it even if it has not produced intoxication. See the comments of Ustadh Muham-

mad 'Ali Farkus in his commentary and authentication of *Miftah al-Wusul* of Tilamsani p. 313.

43. Abd Allah ibn 'Umar said, "The prohibition of wine (*khamr*) was revealed while in Medina. That day there were five forms of [intoxicating] drinks. None of them was the grape [wine] drink." Bukhari reported it.

'Umar b. Al-Khattab said during a public address on the pulpit of Allah's messenger ﷺ, "O ye People! Verily the prohibition of wine was revealed, and it is [from] five things: grapes, dates, honey, wheat, and barley. And wine (*khamr*) is whatever interferes with the mind." Bukhari and Muslim reported it.

And Anas b. Malik said, "Surely wine (*khamr*) was prohibited while wine that day was of (made only from) fresh fruit (*busr*) and dried dates (*tamr*)." Bukhari and Muslim reported it.

Anas said, "I used to give drink to Abu 'Ubayda, Abu Talha, and Ubayy b. Ka'b of the wine [made] from flowers and dates. Then someone came to them, and said: "Wine has been prohibited." So Abu Talha said: "Stand, Anas! And pour it out! Pour it out!" Agreed Upon (*muttafaq 'alaihi*) [between Bukhari and Muslim].

On the authority of Ibn 'Umar the Prophet said, "Every producer of drunkenness (*muskir*) is wine (*khamr*). And every producer of drunkenness is forbidden (*haram*)." Muslim reported it. And khamr is whatever produces drunkenness from the juice of grapes, or [it is] general, just like [the word] *khamrah*. It is also considered masculine [in gender]. And, the general application (*'umum*) is more correct, because it was prohibited when there was no grape wine in Medina, and their drinks were from fresh fruit and dates. It was called *khamr* because it clouds the mind and bars it, or because it interferes with the mind. That is, it mixes with it.

44. Translator: A word that is *mushtarak* in Arabic is one that bears more than one *figurative meaning*. In a sense, it is a synonym of the word *mujmal* (ambiguous). 'Abd Al-'Ali Nizam al-Din al-Ansari defines *mushtarak* as the word "whose meanings are numerous and designed for each [of the various meanings] originally [without any consideration that it has been designed for one particular meaning before]" (*Fawatih al-Rahmut*: p. 261).

Also see the discussion of *mushtarak* in Tilamsani's *Miftah* pp. 508-510 and 519-523.

45. Translator: A word that is *mujmal* is one that has more than one *base meaning*, but one is not able to determine which of those meanings the original meaning intended is unless it is clarified by something else. Refer to *Miftah al-Wusul* pp. 438-468 for a detailed look on the subject of *mujmal*.

46. Translator: This is taken from *Surah al-Baqarah* 2: 187.

47. Abu Ghassan Muhammad b. *Mutarraf* related to us. He said, "Abu Hazim related to us from Sahl b. Sa'd. He said: "*Eat and Drink until the white thread becomes distinct to you from the black thread*" was revealed. But, "*of the dawn*" had not yet come down. So whenever some people wanted to fast, one of them would tie around his leg a white thread and a black thread. And he would continue to eat until he could see both of them. Then Allah afterwards revealed "*of the dawn.*" So they knew that it meant 'the night' and 'the daytime.'" Bukhari reported it.

48. Translator: I was not able to identify who Ibn Taymiyah may have been referring to who could have held this view. Al-Fayyumi mentions in his *Misbah* p. 350, "The '*yad*' is feminine in gender. And it is from the shoulder to the tips of the fingers." So it is translated in this case as the 'arm.' Al-Fayruzabadi says in his *Qamus* p. 1212, "The '*yad*' is the palm (*kaff*). Or [it is] from the tips of the fingers to the palm."

49. Translator: A person is not a native of the language if he is not a Sahabi or one with an understanding of the language as profound as those from the Sahabah, people like the 4 Imams, Sibawayh, and other great linguists. One should not think that just because a person is from an Arab country that he automatically is proficient in the Arabic language. This is one of the greatest misconceptions. Just as most native speakers of English are not scholars of English grammar and etymology, the same can be said for Arabs, Persians, and the peoples of every culture. In all actuality, the people who exerted the most effort to preserve the pristine form of the Arabic language historically have been non-Arabs, Persians in particular. Refer to Ibn Khaldun's '*Muqaddimah*' pp. 466-467 in 'Section 43: Regarding the Fact that The Bearers of Knowledge in Islam, The Majority of them

are the Non-Arabs.' The same can be said for all the other Islamic sciences historically. That is, it was the non-Arabs who did more to preserve the Islamic sciences than the Arabs throughout Islamic history.

50. Translator: Another example of this is how the Shafi'is and Hanafis differ over whether or not the testimony of a person who is guilty of accusing a woman of illicit intercourse can be accepted after repenting from the sin. Allah says of such people, *And do not accept a testimony of theirs ever. And those are the openly defiant ones [all] save those who have repented...* [Nur: 4-5]. The first part of the quote is general, *And do not accept a testimony of theirs ever. And those are the openly defiant ones.* The statement necessitates two things for such people: [1] that the testimony of those guilty and punished for calumny of women should never be accepted, and [2] that they are labeled as '*openly defiant*' (*fasiqun*). The next part of the quote specifies this generality by saying, *...[all] save those who have repented...* The Shafi'is apply the exception to both the matter of restoring the credibility of the person as well as removing from him the label of being one who is openly defiant against God's commands. But Hanafis apply the exception only to the part that removes the label of the person being an open defiant (*fasiq*). This is all due to the disagreement over whether or not the general expression that has some of its constituents excluded ('*amma makhsus*) still maintains its general authority once specification enters into it. See *Miftah al-Wusul* pp. 529-538.

51. Translator: What this is likely referring to is what is called *mafhum al-mukhalafa* (contrast indication). This is when one infers and deduces a legal ruling from a statement where the ruling is not directly mentioned. But, one merely understands that when the thing mentioned in the report has an opposite, that that opposite is applied in contradistinction to ruling established. For example, scholars hold the view that the father of a young lady who has reached puberty may marry her without her consent based on the statement of the Prophet e, "The deflowered woman (*thayyib*) has more right over herself than her guardian does." In other words, the woman who has been married before may not be married to a man without her consent. And the opposite of a woman who has lost her virginity through marriage is

one who has not been married nor has lost her virginity. So the hadith does not apply to the latter. Consequently, scholars have ruled that a father may marry such a girl without her consent. The overwhelming majority of legal theorists hold by the rule of contrast indication (*mafhum al-mukhalafa*). Hanafis, however, do not consider it to be authoritative in spite of the fact that they still rule the same as the majority does in this particular issue based on other sources. See *Miftah al-Wusul* pp. 552-568.

52. Translator: The overwhelming majority of legal theorists (*usuli-yun*) are of the view that when a scriptural text comes as a general expression but related to a specific incident, it can be applied to other cases that fall under the generality. Others hold the view that it can only be applied according to the specific case. An example of this is that once one of the Sahabah asked the Prophet ﷺ during the Hajj about which mount they should begin the *sa'y* with, and he said, "Start with the one that Allah started with." Shafi'i used this as proof that one must perform lustrations (*wudu*) in the sequence that the Prophet ﷺ did. However, some objected to this saying that this statement was made with reference to the Hajj, not *wudu*. And even though the statement is general, it may only be used with respect to the situation he said it in. See *Miftah al-Wusul* along with Ustadh Farkus' comments on pp. 539-541.

53. Translator: Most legal theorists hold the view that a verbal command in Arabic outwardly indicates that the action being ordered is compulsory. The unpopular view about Shafi'i is that he considered it to outwardly indicate nothing more than that the act is recommended. Although, the command may indicate a host of other things, like neutrality, intimidation, belittlement, general direction, and others, it cannot be redirected from its original indication without strong evidence. For this narration about Shafi'i, this would mean that none of these other meanings may apply to it without evidence. And that it can indicate something other than a recommendation only with that evidence. But the more popular narration is that Shafi'i held that the imperative stripped of any qualifiers indicates obligation, as the majority. See *Al-Mustasfa* p. 759 and *Miftah al-Wusul* with the comments of Ustadh Muhammad 'Ali Farkus p. 375. As for the other question of if the imperative stripped of any qualifiers

indicates that the thing ordered is to be carried out immediately or with delay, scholars have also differed about this. As a result, the opinion of most Hanafis is that when a person has the means to make the Hajj, it must be carried out without delay, while the Shafi'is say the opposite. Both views are found in the Maliki School. Imam Sahnun and the western Malikis hold the same view as the Shafi'is, while Ibn al-Qassar and the eastern Malikis hold the view of the Hanafis. See *Miftah al-Wusul* with the comments of Farkus p. 381.

54. Translator: The definite article 'the' (*al* in Arabic) sometimes indicates that the noun that it is attached to is something familiar (*li al-'ahd*). But at times, it is used to indicate a general category or generality (*istighraq al-jins*) as in Allah's saying, *Verily man is in loss*. That is, the category of *man*, not a specific man. This sometimes complicates the proper understanding of some scriptural quotes, since some scholars may interpret the definite article as referring to familiar thing, while others may interpret it as a reference to a general category of things.

55. Translator: Or verbs.

56. Translator: The point here is very difficult to understand.

57. Translator: Imam al-Jurjani defines '*muqtada al-nass*' (the expression with pursuant meaning) as, "That [meaning] which the words do not [directly] point to and is not uttered. However, it is—from the immediate result of the utterance—more general than being scriptural (*shar'iyan*) or rational (*'aqliyan*). And it has been said, 'it is an expression of making what is not spoken to be something that is spoken in order to rectify what has been spoken.' An example of it is [Allah's saying regarding the atonement for certain sins], …*Then the freeing of a slave*. It is pursuant legally and scripturally that it (the slave) is to be one that is owned [by another], since there is no manumission [permitted] with regard to what the son of Adam (humans) do not own. Such [words] are to be added so that the assumption made from the words are, …*Then, the freeing of a slave in one's ownership* (*fa tahriru raqabatin mamluka*). See *Kitab al-Ta'rifat* p. 226.

58. Translator: That is, the source books on legal theory do not cover every single point of disagreement.

59. Translator: This is like the difference of opinion between the majority of scholars and many of the Hanafis regarding whether or not the general statements found in the Quran can be given specification by non-concurrent reports (*khabar al-wahid*) from the hadith. The majority holds it to be permissible, while Hanafis hold it to be permissible only when the indications found in the Quranic verses are weak in their indication and specification is given through an additional text. Only in such a situation can they be specified by non-concurrent reports. Based on this difference, they differed over Allah's saying *Made unlawful for you are carrion...* [Ma'idah: 3] The majority gave specification to this generalisation by the Prophet's statement ﷺ about the water of the ocean, "Its water is pure. Its carrion is lawful." Hanafis respond that since this report is not supported by another similar or more convincing than it, it cannot be used to give specification to the Quranic verse. And since the Quran is weightier of a proof than the non-concurrent report, it is acted upon and the report is discarded with. See *Miftah al-Wusul* pp. 534-536.

60. Translator: An example of this is the fact that most scholars agree that when the topic and ruling of two texts is the same, and one is unqualified while the other is qualified, the unqualified text must be interpreted according to the one that is qualified. An example of this is the hadith that says, "There is no marriage without a guardian, a dower, and two witnesses." Another version of the hadith says, "There is no marriage without a guardian, a dower, and two witnesses of good repute." The majority of scholars construe the first hadith according to the meaning of the second. Consequently, they make it a condition that the two witnesses of the marriage must be of good repute and integrity (*shahiday 'adl*). Abu Hanifah, however, does not accept the authenticity of the hadith. So he rules that the two witnesses can be an openly defiant sinner (*fasiq*). This is the case when the topic and ruling pertain to the same matter. But when the topic and ruling pertain to two different things, most scholars agree that the unqualified text should not be construed according to the purport of the one that is qualified, as in one's attempt to define the limits of the hand/arm that should be cut when combining between Allah's saying, *And the thief male and female, sever their hands* [Ma'idah: 38] and His order to wash

the hands to the elbows [Ma'idah: 6]. As for when the topic of the two texts is different while the judgment passed in its regard is the same, some Malikis hold the view that the unqualified is to be construed according to the qualified when another qualifying element exists (*bi jami'*), while others among them hold that it can be qualified by it even without an additional qualifying element (*bi ghayri jami'*). Hanafis disagree with applying this rule when the subjects of the two texts are different. For this reason, Malikis use Allah's saying concerning the atonement for unintentional murder ...*then, the freeing of a believing slave* [Nisa: 92] to qualify His saying regarding the pre-Islamic practice of divorcing one's wife by declaring her to be one's mother (*zihar*) ...*then the freeing of a slave before they touch one another* [Mujadalah: 3]. Hanafis disagree on the basis that the topics of the two texts are dissimilar. See *Miftah al-Wusul* pp. 541-549.

61. Translator: This is like in Allah's saying, *And when you have concluded the sacred rites of the pilgrimage, hunt* [Ma'idah: 2]. 'Hunt' is a command. The initial indication of a command is that the thing ordered is an obligation. But since we know from other sources that hunting is not a religious obligation, the effect of the command is no more than an indication of permissibility.

62. Translator: This is like Allah's saying, *Allah's hand is over their hand* [Al-Fath: 10]. The hand is a limb of the body and a tool utilised by human beings to grasp, strike, touch, and other things. And since Allah said, *There is nothing like unto Him* [Shura: 11] and *He has no complement* [Ikhlas: 4], we know that this is just a figurative expression used by the Creator to indicate something other than the apparent meaning. So, one should not attempt to infer a specific meaning from it, since Allah only knows exactly what He means by it.

63. [It has been reported] on the authority of Ibn 'Abbas that the Messenger of Allah ﷺ said, "The one who is purchasing his freedom (*mukatab*) is manumitted according to how much he has paid. And the determined punishment (*hadd*) is implemented against him according to how much he has been manumitted. And he is given of the inheritance according to how much he has been manumitted." Tirmidhi reported it and said: "A fair hadith (*hasan*)."

64. Refer to *Jala Al-Afham fi al-Salati 'ala khayr al-Anam 'alayhi al-Salatu wa al-Salam* of Ibn Al-Qayim Al-Jawziyah.

65. Translator: This is the view of the Hanafis. See *Usul al-Shashi* pp. 284-286.

66. Translator: This is another Hanafi view. But Hanafis actually rejected this hadith because in their view it contradicts with a stronger hadith (*sunnah mashhurah*) wherein the Prophet ﷺ states, "The burden of proof is on the claimant. And the oath is on the denier." And when a non-concurrent report (*khabar al-wahid*) conflicts with a *sunnah mashhurah*, they act on the latter and abandon the former. See *Usul al-Shashi* pp. 280-283.

67. Translator: This is a reference to Malikis.

68. Translator: This is a reference to the prophetic tradition, "The two parties of a sale are with the option [of completing or canceling the transaction], as long as they do not part company." The majority of scholars deduce from this that if two people are involved in a business transaction, they have the option of canceling the transaction as long as they are still in one another's company, even if they have begun to discuss a different topic. Malikis, on the other hand, hold that once the item and cost are exchanged and the two parties begin to discuss a separate matter, there is no option given to either of them to cancel the transaction for refund, unless it is something they freely agree to. The opinion of the majority necessitates that it is a right of both parties to get a refund as long as they are in one another's presence. But Malikis interpret "…as long as they have not parted company…" as 'parting in words,' not 'physical presence.' For a detailed discussion of this matter refer to Ibn Daqiq al-'Id's *Ihkam al-Akham Sharh 'Umdat al-Ahkam* 3/102-109.

69. Translator: The hadith concerning the option of refund as long as the two parties have not parted one another's company was challenged by Malikis, Hanafis, Ibrahim Al-Nakha'i, and all the Seven Fuqaha of Medina with the exception of Said b. al-Musayyab. The majority of scholars, which include the Shafi'is, the Hanbalis, and Ibn Habib and 'Abd Al-Hamid Al-Saigh from the Malikis, grant more authority to the hadith. See *Tamhid* 14/1511, *Sharh 'Umdat al-Ahkam* 4/5, *Fath Al-Bari* 5/233, and *Mawahib Al-Jalil* 4/310.

70. Translator: We have already spoken about the Hanafi opposition to certain hadiths base on legal analogy.

71. Translator: This here is a very important statement to make. For it shows humility in face of the possibility that Ibn Taymiyah might be wrong in his views and his belief that in some instances the scholars did not have strong enough evidence to abandon the hadith in the cases they did.

72. Translator: The reader should keep in mind that these arguments posited by Ibn Taymiyah are directed at scholars, especially those who have reached the level of *ijtihad*. They are not directed at non-*mujtahid* scholars and laypeople, since such people do not have the capacity to distinguish between what is sound and weak, what is abrogated and not abrogated, and the rules of interpretation of scripture. As for the non-scholar, his duty is to follow the legitimate *ijtihad* of his Imam even if he is confronted with a hadith that apparently is contravened by his Imam. His duty is to seek out the reason that his Imam did not act upon the hadith. If it happens that it was due to not knowing it and the scholars of his school have adopted a standard view in the school that supports the hadith, then the non-scholar is to act upon it, not whenever someone brings him a hadith, be it scholar or non-scholar. As for scholars qualified to do *ijtihad*, it is impermissible for them to follow the *ijtihad* of another *mujtahid* after reaching a conclusion based on his/her scholarly endeavor (*ijtihad*). (Refer to Ghazali's *Al-Mustasfa*' p. 611-619) This is because the views expressed by the *mujtahid* are tantamount to him saying that Allah's verdict in the matter is *such and such* as he states. This means that the *mujtahid* must believe that his view is as Allah has judged it to be, since only Allah can legislate. And the *mujtahid* merely clarifies and removes the veil of the unknown ruling for us.

73. Translator: Bear in mind that Ibn Taymiyah is not making this statement in the same context that many people today use it when they say that the Quran and the Sunnah are infallible while the opinions of the four Imams are fallible. This is clearly not his intent because of everything he already said and every justification he has given for scholars contravening sound hadiths. Yes! The Quran and Sunnah as sources of law and guidance are infallible and are more reliable than the opinions of

scholars with respect to authenticity and transmission. But the Quran and Sunnah do not spell everything out for us in clear terms. And if it had not been for that, there would be no opinion of a scholar. Everything would have been revelation. So when scholars move to interpret the Quran and the Sunnah and then differ with one another, one scholar's opinion or view is not necessarily more superior to another's as long as the basis for his opinion has some portion of due consideration and relies on valid and pertinent theories, concepts, and realities.

74. Translator: In other words, were we to accept that the proofs of scripture are subject to error, we could cancel out their authority at will until we no longer find any use for them.

75. Translator: That is, we are pardoned for not following the scholar who abandons the hadith in spite of knowing it.

76. Translator: What people must understand is that the early Imams did not view the *sahih hadith* in the same light that many of us do today. Many Muslims today consider a *sahih hadith* to be a 100% factual report, when in fact it is not a 100% factual report unless it is *mutawatir* (a report of concurrent chains/indisputable transmission). Otherwise, it is *most likely* factual. In other words, due to the degree of doubt that still exists regarding the basic *sahih hadith*, the early scholars saw that there remained room for other sources to be able to produce a higher degree of certainty than even certain *sahih hadiths* that were not *mutawatir*. For this reason, none of them contravened or preferred anything over a *sahih hadith* that was *mutawatir*. This preference or abandonment only happened with respect to *non-mutawatir sahih hadiths*. This is because—despite our acceptance that the transmitters in a *sahih* chain happen to be truthful and precise in what they relate from memory, we still do not deem it impossible for them to lie, forget, or make a mistake in a hadith. This is where the doubt enters. But in spite of this doubt, there is no reason for us to doubt the veracity and accuracy of the transmitters in a *sahih* chain, because if one is not known to lie on normal occasions or to forget what he has heard, then it is not likely that he lied or forgot in a case like the narration of the hadith. So our Imams, like Malik and Abu Hanifah, did not reject *sahih hadiths* or claim them to be false. They just considered certain other sources or principles to be stronger, giving greater

certainty than those *sahih hadiths* they chose not to act upon. So Ibn Taymiyah's championing of the hadith is merely a result of his own orientation as a Hanbali scholar and limited *mujtahid* in his own right. So one should not take his words as a condemnation or retraction from what he already made mention of with respect to the excuses he gave for the different Imams and the reasons for them not acting upon *sahih hadiths*.

77. He is Bishr b. Abu Karimah 'Abd Al-Rahman Al-Murisi who was an 'Adawi by slave patronage (*wala*) Abu 'Abd Al-Rahman, the Mu'tazili jurist acquainted with philosophy. He was the head of the Murisi faction who adopted the view of *Irja'* (Translator: i.e. the view that sins do not harm anyone and that every Muslim will go straight to Heaven regardless of his misdeeds). And it was ascribed to him. He learned law (*fiqh*) from Qadi Abu Yusuf. He adopted the view of the *Jahmiyah* (Translator: i.e. the view that Allah is stripped of all His positive attributes like power, knowledge, speech, etc. but that He is given all His names), and he was persecuted during the reign of Harun Al-Rashid. It was said: His father was a Jew. He has a number of works. And Darimi has the book, *The Dissolution of Bishr Al-Murisi* regarding the rebuttal against his school (*madhhab*). He died in the year (218 a.h./ 833 c.e.).

78. Translator: This narration is one of the clearest examples of how there can be an explicit or near explicit statement of the Prophet – may Allah bless and grant him peace, while some might still find reason to not obey the outward meaning of it due to some other consideration. This is exactly what happens many times with the Imams. And even though we may not know their evidence, we are not to necessarily question their judgments that have been accepted by those after them.

79. Translator: The overwhelming majority of scholars permit using legal analogy to give specification to the Quran. The Hanafis, however, only allow it when a Quranic verse gives specification first in some weak form, similar to their view regarding the use of non-concurrent reports to specify the general words of the Quran. See *Miftah al-Wusul* p. 536.

80. Translator: A *sa'* is an ancient measure for grain, which originally denoted four times the amount of grain that one could hold

in one's hands while putting them together. In terms of volume, it is approximately 4.212 liters. See W. Hinz, *Islamische Masse und Gewichte* (Leiden, 1970) pp. 45-46 for the definition of the *muddu* (= 1.053 liters), which Nafrawi defines as "the heaping amount both hands held together can hold" (*al-Fawakih al-Dawani* 1/366). The *sa'* is equal to four *muddus*.

81. On the authority of Abu Sa'id Al-Khudri and on the authority of Abu Hurayrah ؓ that Allah's Messenger ﷺ made a man the governor of Khaybar. So, he brought him dates of the highest quality (*janib*). So the Messenger of Allah ﷺ said, "Are all the dates of Khaybar like this?" He said: "No. By Allah! O Messenger of Allah! We take the *Sa'* of this for two *Sa's* [of that] and two *Sa's* for three." So the Messenger of Allah ﷺ said, "Do not do [that]! Sell the batch [of the*m*] for *dirhams*. Then, purchase with dirhams those of high quality." Bukhari reported it.

82. On the authority of Abu Sa'id Al-Khudri and on the authority of Abu Hurayrah ؓ that Allah's Messenger ﷺ made a man governor over Khaybar. He, then, came to him with dates of excellent quality (*janib*). Allah's Messenger ﷺ said: "Are all the dates of Khaybar like these?" He said: "O Allah's Messenger! Verily we take one *Sa'* of this for two *Sa's*, and [we give] two *Sa's* for three." So the Messenger of Allah ﷺ said: "Do not do this! Sell a batch with silver currency (*dirhams*), and then buy the good quality [dates] with *dirhams*." Bukhari reported it.

83. The hadith has a severed chain. Daraqutni reported it as well as Ibn Majah. Abu Dawud reported it from the hadith of Awza'i. And Hakim, Ibn Khuzaymah, and Ibn Hibban reported it from the hadith of Al-Walid b. 'Ubayd b. Abu Rabah from his paternal uncle from 'Ata from Ibn 'Abbas to the Prophet (*marfu'*). The hadith also has numerous chains by which it is strengthened. And Abu Dawud reports it with the wording, "We went out on a journey and a rock struck a man among us and opened up a wound in his head. Then he had a wet dream, and then asked his companions: "Do you find for me any license to do dry lustrations (*tayammum*)?" They said: "We find no license for you…" to the end. Its chain is severed.

84. Translator: It is important to mention here that Ibn Taymiyah

deems this hadith to be sufficient evidence for arguing the point that only those with the conditions of *ijtihad* may issue fatwa despite the fact that scholars differ about the soundness of this report. But if the report is sound, it stands as one of the strongest proofs of how one may have knowledge of the Sunnah and *sahih hadiths* but still lack the qualifications to speak on Islam authoritatively. So having only *Sahih al-Bukhari, Muslim*, or any other Sahih is not sufficient for one to live his life as a Muslim and to gain a full and complete understanding of how the law works without taking refuge with the living scholars and studying with them the books of *fiqh*. This also makes it clear that Ibn Taymiyah's earlier comments about not preferring the opinions of scholars over the scriptural proofs when they are in conflict are directed at scholars, not at laymen. Laymen always have to take refuge with the opinions of scholars, even if they find hadiths that apparently conflict with the views of their *mujtahid* Imam. One either has to follow his own scholar's interpretation of the hadith or his own. If you do the first, you are absolved from sin. But if you do the second, you are like those who gave fatwa to the one with the head wound who were condemned by Allah's Messenger e.

85. On the authority of Usamah b. Zayd b. Harithah y, he said, "The Messenger of Allah ﷺ dispatched us to Al-Hurqah from Juhaynah. So we met them at dawn and we defeated them. Then I and another man from the Ansar caught up to a man from amongst them. So once we cornered him, he said: "*La ilaha illa Allah*." So the Ansari withdrew from him, and I stabbed him with my spear until I killed him. Then once we returned, that reached the Prophet e." He said to me, "O Usamah! Did you kill him after he said: *La ilaha illa Allah*?!" I said: O Messenger of Allah! He was only trying to protect himself!" He said, "Did you kill him after he said: *La ilaha illa Allah*?!!!" He continued to repeat it until I wished that I had not accepted Islam before that day." Bukhari reported it.

Al-Huraqat—with a domma on the *ha* and a *fatha* on the *ra*—is an under-tribe (*butn*) from *Juhaynah*. Its leader was Ghalib b. 'Ubayd Allah Al-Kalbi. And their homes were beyond the under-tribe of *Nakhlah* from the land of *Banu Murrah*. As for the one Usamah killed, he was Mirdas b. Nuhaik.

86. Translator: In other words, before we can say that guilt can truly be attributed to the scholar for abandoning the hadith for his own opinion, it must be determined that he knowingly and insolently rebelled against the Prophet's words and that he did not have any of the 10 aforementioned valid excuses for not acting on the hadith in accord with whatever methodology he adopts.

87. Translator: Jalal al-Din Al-Mahalli says about *Istidlal*: "It is a proof which is not a text (Quran and Sunnah), not unanimous consensus (*ijma'*), and not legal analogy (*qiyas*)." This is like the various types of legal analogies discussed in the discipline of logic (*mantiq*), like *al-qiyas al-iqtirani, al-qiyas al-istithna'i,* and *qiyas al-'aks*. [*Jam' al-Jawami'*: 2/343-344].

88. The Messenger of Allah ﷺ said, "The judges are three: one in the Garden and two in the Fire. So as for he who is in the Garden, he is a man who knew the truth and gave a verdict in accord with it. And a man who knew the truth and was unjust in his verdict, he is in the Fire. And a man who gave a verdict to people while being ignorant, he is in the Fire." Abu Dawud reported it in *Kitab Al-Aqdiyah*. And Ibn Majah reported it in *Kitab al-Ahkam* on the authority of Buraydah.

89. Translator: Shaykh Muhammad Fayd al-Hasan al-Gangohi says about Imam Al-Shashi's saying about the non-concurrent report (And it obligates acting by it in the rulings of the sacred law), "That is, the ruling of the non-concurrent report (*khabar al-wahid*) is that it obligates action, but it does not obligate knowledge (*'ilm*), neither definitive knowledge (*'ilm al-yaqin*) nor confidence producing knowledge (*'ilm al-tama'nina*). This is the view of most of the people of knowledge and the generality of the jurists. However, Ahmad and most of the scholars of hadith held that it produces definitive knowledge. But, this is contrary to what we find in our souls from non-concurrent reports." (*'Umdat al-Hawashi* p. 274) Abu Hamid al-Ghazali says, "And what has been narrated concerning the scholars of hadith in that that obligates knowledge, then perhaps they meant that it produces knowledge of the obligation of acting [in accord to it in legal matters], since [one's] 'assumption' (*zann*) is sometimes called 'knowledge' (*'ilm*). Because of this, some of them said: "It produces outward knowledge (*'ilm zahir*)." But, knowledge does not have an outward and an inward.

Rather, such is no more than assumption (*zann*)." (*Al-Mustasfa min 'Ilm al-Usul* 1/433-434)

90. Translator: Some scholars stipulate a particular number of transmitters in order for a report to produce definitive knowledge and, thus, be considered indisputably authentic (*mutawatir*). Numbers like 5, 12, 20, 40, 70, 313, and others have been suggested as the minimum numbers required in order for a report to produce 100% authenticity. See *Amidi's Al-Ihkam fi Usul al-Ahkam: Juz* 2/268.

91. In another version, "I and Umm Mahabbah went out. Then we entered upon 'Aisha and greeted her with peace. She said: "Who are you?" We said: "From the People of Kufah." She (the narrator) said: "Then it was as if she turned away from us." So Umm Mahabbah said to her: "O Mother of the Faithful! I used to have a slave girl and I sold her to Zayd b. Arqam, the Ansari, for 800 *dirhams* until he pays it [later]. Then he wanted to sell her [back to me on the spot]. So I bought her from him for 600 *dirhams* on the spot (*naqdan*)." Then 'Aishah said: "Evil is what you have purchased! And evil is what you have sold! Inform Zayd that his striving with Allah's Messenger is null unless he repents…" As for the hadith above, Daraqutni reported it on the authority of Yunus from his mother, Bint Anfa'. Daraqutni recorded it in *Kitab al-Mu'talif wa al-Mukhtalif* where he said: "On the authority of Umm Mahabbah that a woman relates from 'Aishah y. Abu Ishaq Al-Sabi'i related her hadith from his wife, Al-'Aliyah. And Yunus b. Ishaq also related it from Umm Al-'Aliyah Bt. Anfa' from Umm Mahabbah from 'Aishah y. And he said: "Umm Mahabbah and Al-'Aliyah are unknown. They are not to be presented as proof. And Imam Ahmad also reported the hadith in his *Musnad* saying: "Its chain is *jayyid* (i.e. between *hasan* and *sahih*)." Ibn Al-Jawzi said, "They said: "Al-'Aliyah is unknown. She is not to be advanced as proof. And her reports are not accepted." We say: "Rather, she is a well-known woman of splendid status. Ibn Sa'd mentioned her in *Al-Tabaqat*. He said: "Al-'Aliyah Bt. Anfa' b. Shurahil is the wife of Abu Ishaq Al-Sabi'i. She heard from 'Aishah y.""

92. Translator: Imam Nawwawi says, "And the scholars have agreed upon the permissibility of acting on the weak hadiths that con-

tain encouragement toward good virtuous actions." [*Sharh al-Arba'in al-Nawwawiyya:* p. 3]

93. Translator: This is like the legal maxim supported by Malikis and many other scholars that 'when the lawful and unlawful unite, the unlawful is granted victory,' which means that whenever one text forbids a thing and another allows it, judgment should be given in favour of the prohibition out of caution. See Suyuti's *Ashbah wa Naza'ir* p. 74, Ibn Nujaym's *Ashbah wa Naza'ir* p. 121, Iraqi's *al-Taqyid wa al-Idah* p. 282, and Dr. Muhammad Rugi's *Qawa'id al-Fiqh al-Islami* p. 274.

94. Bukhari reported it in *Kitab al-Buyu'* (The Book of Sales). Muslim reported it in *Kitab al-Musaqat,* just as Abu Dawud, Tirmidhi, Nasa'i, and Ibn Majah reported it. And the meaning of '*ha – ha*' is 'This' (*hadha*). It is stated with *alif mamdudah* and with *alif maqsurah*. But the *mamdudah* is more popular.

95. Imam Ahmad and Nasa'i reported it. And Muslim reported in *Kitab al-Musaqat*: "Whatever is delayed is interest. So return it."

96. The chain of the hadith is sound (*sahih*). Imam Ahmad related it in his *Musnad*. And Abu Dawud, Tirmidhi, and Ibn Majah reported it.

97. Abu Dawud reported it in *Kitab al-Ashribah*. And Imam Ahmad reported it in his *Musnad* on the authority of Ibn 'Abbas with the words, "I heard Allah's messenger ﷺ say: "Gabriel came to me and said: "O Muhammad! Verily Allah has cursed wine, the squeezer of it, the presser of it, the drinker of it, the carrier of it, the one it is carried to, the seller of it, the buyer of it, the one who gives it for drink, and the one who asks to be given it to drink." And Ibn Majah reported it on the authority of Anas b. Malik. Mundhiri said, "Its transmitters are reliable."

98. Bukhari and Muslim reported it with the words, "Every intoxicant is wine. And every intoxicant is forbidden." Tirmidhi, and Nasa'i reported it in *Kitab al-Ashribah*. And Malik reported it in *Muwatta* in *Kitab al-Dahaya*.

99. This view was held by Imam Abu Hanifah.

100. He ﷺ said, "Whatever is delayed is interest. So return it." Muslim reported it.

101. In one version, "May Allah curse the Jews (three times)…" Bukhari reported it in *Kitab al-Anbiya*, Muslim did in *Kitab al-Musaqat*, Abu Dawud in *Kitab al-Buyu'*, Ibn Majah in *Kitab al-Ashribah*, and Darimi in *Kitab al-Ashribah* also.

102. Ibn Juzay al-Kalbi states in his *al-Qawanin al-Fiqhiyyah* p. 130 "It is not lawful for a Muslim to sell wine to a Muslim or non-Muslim and not to sell grapes to one who makes wine from them."

103. Ibn Hajar states in his *Fath* 11/571, "And among them (the scholars) are those who permitted hair extensions absolutely whether it be with other hair or with something that is not hair when it is with the husband's knowledge and his permission."

104. Bukhari and Muslim reported it.

105. Agreed Upon

106. Translator: This battle was between 'Ali's forces and 'Aishah's. See Ibn Kathir's *al-Bidayah wa al-Nihayah* p. 319.

107. Translator: This battle was between 'Ali and Mu'awiyah. See Ibn Kathir's *al-Bidayah wa al-Nihayah* p. 351.

108. Translator: That is, their good deeds prevent them from going to Hell because of fighting one another.

109. Bukhari and Muslim reported it from the hadith of Abu Dharry.

110. Imam Ahmad and Nasa'i reported it. Tirmidhi declared it to be sound. And Ibn Majah reported it from the hadith of 'Uqbah b. 'Amir y.

111. Nawwawi ascribes this view to Said b. al-Musayyab. See *Sharh Sahih Muslim* 5/2 p. 4.

112. Translator: What this means is that as long as the chief elements of the marriage exist (consent, dower, witnesses, and the guardian—according the majority), the marriage is not invalidated by the conditions added to the marriage contract. Similarly, if either the dower or one of the spouses is not specified, the contract would be validated upon whoever is designated of marriageable spouses and whatever dower is given to the woman by the man as long as it meets the requirements of the Shariah in the case when the option is given to the man to give whatever dower he would like. This applies as long as there is no agree-

ment that the marriage will occur without a dower. In such a case, the marriage would be invalid.

113. Agreed upon. And Abu Dawud reported it from the hadith of Sa'd b. Abi Waqqas and Abu Bakrah y.

114. Muslim reported it.

115. Translator: Some have used the hadith: "The child belongs to the bed. And for the adulterer is the stone (or nothing)" as evidence supporting the idea that children born out of wedlock before Islam cannot be claimed as one's legitimate children and that one has no responsibility toward them or any right over them. Some have used it for this in spite of the fact that the hadith clearly relates to a separate matter, which is the matter of 'who will be given responsibility for and custody of a child who a dying man happens to claim paternity for as a result of an adulterous relationship with the child's mother.' This is what the hadith relates to, not to the above matter. So, if a man has children before Islam as the result of illicit intercourse, he has no right to deny his paternity for that child as long as he has acknowledged it. And there is nothing in Islam that requires him to do so, in addition to the fact that it goes against the spirit of Islam that encourages the care for orphans, the poor, and the weak. On the other hand, if a Muslim man happens to conceive a child out of wedlock, such a child will not be given the same rights and responsibilities of a legitimate child born through marriage or the like toward its biological father. In other words, the child cannot be ascribed to its biological father (i.e. take his last name), it cannot inherit from him and he cannot inherit from it. He is not obligated to care for it monetarily, although it is encouraged. He has no custody rights over it. The child is not obligated to provide for its biological father if he happens to be poor and the child happens to be rich. And the father is also not obligated to do so, although it is recommended. These rules exist as an added preventive measure to illicit intercourse, the mixing up and confusion of people's lineages, and all the other evils that result from illicit relationships. It is also based on hadiths like the one wherein the Prophet ﷺ said, "What is made lawful through the lawful (*halal*) is not made lawful through the unlawful (*haram*)." From this, the Maliki scholars coin the rule: "What is non-ex-

istent according to scripture is the same as what is non-existent in actuality."

116. Translator: These comments clearly shows the respect Ibn Taimiyah had for the different methodological approaches of the other Imams, although he disagrees with them in declaring certain principles and sources to be stronger than certain hadiths. This is because he championed the methodological approach of Imam Ahmad b. Hanbal. These comments of his show that he believed that the methodological approaches of the other *mujtahid* Imams were legitimate approaches. He only preferred the approach of Imam Ahmad.

117. Translator: An issue that scholars anciently have differed over is the question of whether or not the truth is only one, such that only one opinion is acceptable in the sight of Allah when *mujtahids* differ? Some held the view that all *mujtahids* are correct, and that each variant opinion is accepted by Allah as being a legitimate and sanctioned view. Another question they differed about was whether or not the *mujtahid* who rules incorrectly is actually sinful? Refer to *Al-Mustasfa* of Imam al-Ghazali for more details 2/541-596.

118. Translator: In other words, just because there is no unanimous agreement that something is a sin, it does not mean that it is automatically permissible to do. Just because scholars differ does not mean that one has the liberty to always go with the opinion authorising an action. The consensus that Ibn Taymiyah is referring to above is the consensus that difference of opinions among scholars does not make an act to be permissible due to not being unanimously declared to be impermissible. But there is another principle worthy of mention. That principle is that 'There is no objection to what over which there is disagreement.' In other words, if there is no unanimous agreement that a particular act is a sin, one cannot accuse another of being a sinner for doing that act if the accuser happens to believe it to be a sin. This is like when Muslims accuse others of sin for doing things like, shaving or trimming their beards, not wearing a face veil, taking photographs, etc. Were Muslims to apply this rule more often, we would have much less confusion and division.

119. Translator: This is the matter referred to by scholars as 'the mat-

ter of delaying clarification from the time it is required' (*ta'khir al-bayan 'an waqt al-haja*). This was debated during the early years of Islam. And the question was asked, 'Is it possible for the Prophet ﷺ to delay giving any clarification for a thing that he ordered the Muslims to do beyond the time the clarification is needed?' The majority view is that it is not possible, while many of the companions of Abu Hanifah, The Literalists (*ahl al-zahir*), Abu Bakr al-Maruzi, and Abu Bakr al-Sayrafi adopted the view that it was possible. As for delaying the clarification until the time it is needed, there is agreement that such a thing is possible, like for Allah to obligate the Muslims to make *Salat* during a specific time. It is possible for the Messenger to delay the explanation of the prayer until it becomes an obligation to carry out the order. See *Al-Mustasfa* 1/699-710.

120. Translator: The word translated above as 'learn' is the word *'ta'lim'*, which means 'to teach.' I believe it to be a mistake in the copy of the book in my possession. Allah knows best.

121. Translator: In other words, this generalisation applies to every single Muslim without exception.

122. [As for] the beginning of the hadith "May Allah curse the females who visit graves...," Imam Ahmad, Abu Dawud, and Hakim reported it on the authority of Hassan b. Thabit. And he said in *Al-Zawa'id*: "The chain of the hadith of Hassan b. Thabit is sound (*sahih*), and its transmitters are trustworthy." Tirmidhi and Ibn Majah also reported it on the authority of Abu Hurayrah. Tirmidhi said: "A soundly fair hadith (*hasan sahih*)." And the general purport of the hadith (*mujmalihi*), Abu Dawud and Ibn Majah reported it. And Ibn Hibban reported it in his *Sahih* from the version of Abu Salih Badhan, the client of Umm Hani' on the authority of Ibn 'Abbas. And Tirmidhi declared the hadith to be fair. And it has been said: "This Abu Salih is weak according to the scholars of hadith."

123. Translator: Ibn Hajar states in his *Fath* 3/489, "Al-Qurtubi said: "The outward meaning of the context of Umm 'Atiyyah [in her hadith] is that the prohibition [against woman following the biers to the graveyards] is a prohibition of light discouragement (*nahy tanzih*). And it is what the overwhelming majority of the people of knowledge hold to, while Malik inclined toward abso-

lute permissibility. And it is the view of the people of Medina."

124. The Messenger of Allah said, "Cursed is the one who comes to his woman in her backside." Abu Dawud reported it in *Kitab al-Nikah*. And the *mahash* is the plural of *mahasha*. It is the anus (*dubur*). And the hadith, Ahmad, Abu Dawud, and Nasa'i reported it with the same wording we have mentioned in these marginal notes.

125. The chain of the hadith is weak. And Muslim has reported in his *Sahih*: on the authority of Ma'mar e: "The Messenger of Allah ﷺ said: "Whoever monopolises is in error (*khati'*)." And the one in error (*khati'*) is the sinner.

126. Perhaps, this is a reference to the Companion, Kisan Al-Thaqafi, who was a friend of the Prophet ﷺ before he received revelation from the Sham. He met the Prophet ﷺ on the day of the Conquest of Mecca and offered him a drink of wine, but he refused and informed him that it had been forbidden. Upon that, Kisan ordered his servant to sell the wine. Upon hearing that the Prophet ﷺ said, "The one who made drinking it unlawful has also made it unlawful to sell." See *Muwatta: Kitab al-Ashribah* #1643.

127. Agreed upon. And Imam Ahmad, Tirmidhi, and Abu Dawud reported it on the authority of 'Abd Allah b. 'Umar.

128. Muslim reported it.

129. Translator: Nawwawi considers it to be merely disliked (*makruh*) if it is not done out of conceit. See *'Awn al-Ma'bud: Kitab al-Libas, Bab* 25.

130. Bukhari and Muslim reported it just as the authors of the *Sunan* collections reported it on the authority of 'Abd Allah b. 'Umar with the words, "May Allah curse the *wasilah* and the *mustawsilah*." And in one version, "Allah's messenger ﷺ cursed the *wasilah* and the *mawsulah*." Qurtubi said, "To extend it (*wasluhu*) is for other hair to be added to it by which it becomes plentiful."

131. Bukhari and Muslim reported it from the hadith of Umm Salamah.

132. Bukhari and Muslim reported it from the hadith of Thabit b.

Al-Dahhak Al-Ansari with the wording: "Cursing the Believer (*mu'min*) is like killing him."

133. Bukhari reported it in *Al-Adab Al-Mufrad*.

134. Translator: The term '*athar*' is usually used to refer to the reports that come from those below the Prophet's Companions, The Successors (*Tabi'un*). But it is sometimes also used in a more general sense to refer to any report from anyone of the early generations.

135. Abu Dawud and Tirmidhi reported it as well as Ibn Hibban in his *Sahih* on the authority of Ibn 'Abbas with the wording: "Verily a man cursed the wind in the presence of Allah's messenger. So he said, "Do not curse the wind. For surely it is [merely] commanded. Whoever curses something that does not deserve it, the curse returns to him."

136. Allah's messenger said, "May Allah curse wine. May He curse the one who drinks it and the one who gives it to drink…" Abu Dawud reported it in *Al-Ashribah*. And Imam Ahmad reported it in his *Musnad*.

137. Muslim reported it in his *Sahih*. And Nasa'i reported it on the authority of 'Ali with the wording: "May Allah curse he who curses his parents. May Allah curse he who slaughters for other than Allah. May Allah curse he who grants shelter to an innovator. And may Allah curse he who alters the way-mark of the Earth."

138. Bukhari and Muslim reported it.

139. Muslim reported it on the authority of Jabir.

140. Imam Ahmad reported it with two [different] chains. One of them is sound (*sahih*).

141. Muslim reported it in his *Sahih* on the authority of Anas b. Malik. And the remainder of the hadith is: "Allah will not accept from him on the Day of Resurrection an exchange or indemnity. And the protection conferred by the Muslims (*dhimma*) is one. The lowest of them walks with it. And whoever makes claim to other than his father or claims clientage to other than his patrons, on him is the curse of Allah, the angels, and all of humanity. Allah will not accept from him on the Day of Resurrection

an exchange or indemnity."

142. Bukhari and Muslim reported it, just as the authors of the *Sunan* collections reported it on the authority of Ibn 'Umar b. Al-Khattab.

143. Muslim reported it in his *Sahih* on the authority of 'Abd Allah b. Mas'ud.

144. Muslim reported it with the wording: "Whoever defrauds is not from us."

145. Agreed upon. And Imam Ahmad, Abu Dawud, and Ibn Majah reported it as, "Whoever makes claim to other than his father and he knows, then Paradise is forbidden for him."

146. Agreed upon. And Imam Ahmad, Tirmidhi, and Abu Dawud reported it on the authority of Al-Ash'ath b. Qays and on the authority of 'Abd Allah b. Mas'ud.

147. Muslim reported it in his *Sahih* on the authority of Abu Umamah.

148. Bukhari reported it in *Al-Adab Al-Mufrad* as Bukhari also reported it as well as Muslim, Abu Dawud, and Tirmidhi with the wording: "One who severs ties will not enter Paradise."

149. Ahmad reported it, just as Tirmidhi, Ibn Majah reported it by way of 'Adi b. Hatim, that he entered upon Allah's messenger while he was reciting: "*They took their learned men and monks as lords instead of Allah,*" and then I said: "Verily they did not worship them." So he said: "On the contrary, surely they make unlawful for them the lawful and they made lawful for them the unlawful, and then they followed them. So that is their worship of them."

150. Imam Abu Hamid al-Ghazali states in his *Al-Mustasfa'*, "They (scholars) are in agreement that whenever the *mujtahid* completes his scholarly endeavour [in a matter] and a particular ruling predominates his mind, it is not permitted for him to uncritically imitate (*yuqallid*) one who opposes him, to act in accord with the view of another, or to abandon his own conclusion. As for when he has not yet exerted effort *(lam yajtahid ba'du)* or reflected [on the evidence] because he is incapable of scholarly endeavour *(ijtihad)* like the layman, then he may uncritically

imitate another. But this individual is not a *mujtihad*. However, he may perhaps be capable of scholarly endeavour in some matters while being incapable in others..." [2/611]

151. In all reality the nomenclature of hadith specialists was not standardised until after the time of the virtuous Imams. During the early period there were basically only two types of hadiths: [1] acceptable, and [2] unacceptable. Beyond that, the four Imams differed about the acceptability and unacceptability of certain narrations.

152. Nawawi says in his *Taqrib* p. 31 in stating the conditions for a sahih hadith, "It is the one whose chain of transmission is connected, via those who are upright and with a firm recollection, absent of irregularity and subtle defects."

153. Imam Tilmisani says, "Know that the transmitter must be upright ('adl) and of firm recollection (dabit)." (Miftah al- Wuuul ila Bina' al-Furu' 'ala al-Usul: p. 322)

154. Most hadiths reported by the Companions are transmitted by meaning only. Imam Suyūtī relates a number of examples of this in his *Tadrīb* pp. 298-301. Among those who have admitted to this practice are Wāthila b. al-Asqa', Hudhayfa b. al-Yaman, Al-Hasan, Ibrahim Al-Nakha'i, Sha'bī, Zuhri and many others. Due to this, we will see later that the early Hanafis made a distinction between the Companions who were known for being scholars and those who were not, and rejected the reports by the latter group when it contradicted the dictates of legal analogy (qiyās).

155. Imam Juwaynī says, "The Hashwiyya (Crypto- Anthropomorphists) from the Hanbalis and the recorders of the hadith held the view that the non-corroborating report of the upright person (khabar al-wahid) produces definitive knowledge. But this is disgraceful! The way to comprehend it is not hidden from an intelligent person." (*Al-Burhan* p. 231)

156. See Juwayni's discussion of *tawatur* (indisputable authenticity) in his *Burhan* pp. 216-222.

157. Muslim #1985

158. Ibn Hajar in Fath *Al-Bari* states that both Ibn Mundhir and Ibn Hazm relate that 'Ali, Abu Hurayra, Salman Al-Farisi, and

Abū Dharr Al-Ghifari all fasted on Fridays. Then he quotes Ibn Hazm as saying, "We know of no one opposing them from the Sahaba." Then Ibn Hajar says, "And the overwhelming majority holds the view that the prohibition is merely indicative of sinless discouragement (tanzih). Malik and Abu Hanifa [have stated]: "It is not disapproved of [to fast Friday]." [Fath Al-Bārī: 1/758]

159. *Muwatta*, Kitab al-Siyam: hadith #699

160. Ibn Hajar quotes Shaykh Al-Dawdi as saying, "Perhaps, the prohibition [of doing so] did not reach Malik." However, to assume this would be inconsistent with his reply that "I have not heard anyone of those who are emulated forbidding [the fast of] it (*Jumu'a*)," since his saying this is clearly in response to the question about the permissibility of fasting Friday. So he was clearly aware of there being some talk of its prohibition. And Allah knows best.

161. Malik also reports that Anas ibn Malik said,"I stood behind Abu Bakr,'Umar,and 'Uthman,and none of them would recite, "*Bismillahir-Rahmanir-Rahim,*" when he started the Salat." [hadith #175]

Other narrations of this same hadith exist, but scholars of hadith like Ibn 'Abd Al-Barr have classified them as '*mudtarib*' (contradictory), since some mention the Prophet, some mention only Abu Bakr and 'Umar. In addition, some narrations clearly negate the recitation of the basmala while others clearly establish it (See Sharh al-Zurqani 'ala al-Muwatta': 1/244-245). And when a hadith is considered '*mudtarib*,' it cannot be acted upon or used as evidence for a legal ruling. In spite of this fact, the quote from Malik above shows that his position was less dependent on the hadith report than it was based on the custom of the scholars of his city.

162. According to Qadi Abū Bakr Ibn Al-'Arabi the companions of Imam Malik applied the hadiths about reciting the *basmala* to the *nawafil* (voluntary prayers). [Ahkam Al-Quran: 1/7]

163. The 'ta'awwudh' is to say, "*A'udhu billahi min Ash-Shaytan nir-Rajim*" (I take refuge with Allah from Satan, the accursed.)

164. *Al-Mudawwana Al-Kubra*: 1/105

165. *Muslim*, Kitāb al-Masājid, Bāb al-Taslīm, hadith #1315

166. Shaykh Ahmed also relates the following quotes in his *Masalik*. First while mentioning the basis of Ibn Abi Zayd's mention of making only one *taslīm*, he says, "[That is] according to the standard view (*mashhūr*) because of the hadith of 'A'isha that, "The Messenger of Allah used to give salam in the Salat one time with his head positioned ahead (*tilqa wajhihi*), and then turn [it] slightly to the right side."

Tirmidhi and Ibn Majah related it, and Abu Hatim, Tahawi, Tirmidhi, Bayhaqi, Daraqutni, Ibn 'Abd Al-Barr, Baghawi, and Nawwawi [all] declared it to be weak. Hafiz [Ibn Hajar] said:

"Hakim was careless, and graded it as sound (sahih)." [This is said also because of] the hadith of Sahl ibn Sa'd that, "The Prophet used to give *salām* one time while keeping his head straight." Ibn Majah related it, and he related the like of it from the hadith of Salama ibn Al-Akwa'. But the chain of each of them is weak. There is also in the chapter [a report] on the authority of Anas with Bayhaqi. Hafiz said, "Its transmitters are trustworthy." But, Bāji and others said: "The hadiths of the one *taslīm* are unfounded (*ghayru thabita*)."

'Aqili said: "Nothing regarding [making] one *taslīm* is sound (sahih)." (*Masalik al-Dilalat Fi Sharh Masa'il al-Risala*: p. 51)

167. Imam Muslim also reports on the authority of Abu Ma'mar that, "An emir in Mecca used to offer two *taslims*, and 'Abd Allah [Ibn 'Umar] said: "And where [or how] did he catch hold of it?" Shaykh Al-Mubarakfuri states in his *Minnat Al-Mun'im Fi Sharh sahih Muslim*: 1/370, "It appears from his comment that this Sunna had been abandoned by practically all of the Imams during that time. So 'Abd Allah was impressed by his knowledge of this Sunna and his adherence to it." I would say that this is more likely a question indicative of 'Abd Allah b. 'Umar's condemnation of this practice, since it has become well-established that Ibn 'Umar used to give one *taslīm*. If practically everyone had abandoned the practice of two *taslims* at that time, then why would Ibn 'Umar be impressed with such a thing if it was the Sunna? For if it was a regular practice of his, the people would have known, and it would have been the commonly acknowledge Sunna. Ibn 'Umar is also considered to be the most tena-

cious of all the Sahaba about adherence to the Sunna. That in itself strengthens the Maliki argument.

168. *Al-Mudawwana Al-Kubra:* 1/165

169. Malik mentions the reports concerning Ibn 'Umar and 'A'isha in his *Muwatta*. The hadith of Ibn 'Umar is,

"On the authority of Nafi', Ibn 'Umar used to say, "Al-Salamu 'alaykum," to his right, and then he would reply to the Imam. If there was someone on his left, he would reply to him [too]."

The idea of offering three *taslīms* if someone is also on a person's left side is also supported by the following hadiths: Samura b. Jundub reports that the Prophet said: "When the Imam gives *salam*, then reply to him." Ibn Majah

In another narration he says, "The Messenger of Allah ordered us to give *salam* to our Imams and that we give *salam* to one another." Abu Dawud & Hakim The version of Bazzar is, "We were ordered to reply to the Imam, to love one another, and to give salām to one another." Bazzar added in Kitab Al-Salat, "Its chain is fair (*hasan*)."

170. *Ibid.*

171. Ibn Wahb and Ibn Al-Qasim said, "On the authority of Malik from Ibn Shihāb from Salim b. 'Abd Allah from his father (Ibn 'Umar) that the Messenger of Allah used to raise his hands parallel with his shoulders when he started the takbīr for the Salat." Waki' [narrated] on the authority of Sufyan Al-Thawri from 'Asim from 'Abd Al-Rahmān b. al-Aswad from

Al-Aswad and 'Alqama [that] they [both] said: "'Abd Allah b. Mas'ud said: "Shall I not lead in the prayer [likened to the prayer] of Allah's Messenger ?" He said: "Then he prayed and raised his hands only once."" Waki' said, "On the authority of Ibn Abi Layla from his brother, 'Isa and Al-Hakam from 'Abd Al-Rahman b. Abi Layla from Al-Bara b. 'Azib that Allah's Messenger used to raise his hands when he started the Salat, and then he would not raise them [again] until he finished." Waki' said, "On the authority of Abu Bakr b. 'Abd Allah b. Qattaf Al-Nahashli from 'Asim ibn Kulayb from his father that 'Ali used to raise his hands when he started the Salat, and then did not repeat [it]." He (Waki') said: "He (Kulayb) had witnessed [the battle of] Siffin with him ('Ali). The companions of Ibn Mas'ud used to raise their hands in the first [takbira], and then they did not repeat [it], and Ibrahim Al-Nakha'i used to do it." (*Al-Mudawwa Al-Kubra:* 1/108)

172. Shaykh Muhammad al-Gangohi says, "Then know that the narration of the non-jurist is rejected when it conflicts with legal analogy only when the Umma has not received him with acceptance. As for when they have received him, he is accepted. Know also that this is the view of 'Isa b. Abban. Qadi Imam Abu Zayd—may Allah show him mercy—chose it also, and most of those of the later days have followed him. As for the view of Shaykh Abu al-Hasan Al-Karkhi—may Allah show him mercy—and those who follow him, it is not a condition in order for the report to be preferred to legal analogy that the transmitter be a jurist. Rather, the report of any upright person is accepted in all circumstances with the condition that it does not contradict the Book and the Sunna Mashhura, because the presumption that the transmitter has altered something after the establishment of his integrity and firm recollection is a baseless assumption. In fact, it is more apparent that he has related the report in the same way he heard it, so if he had changed it, he would have changed it only in a way whereby the meaning has not been altered. This is the more apparent state of those who recall reports and who are upright transmitters, especially from the Sahaba—may Allah be pleased with them. This is due to the fact that they witnessed the textual pronouncements first hand, and they are from the people of the language. So such a report is sound (sahih) according to what is apparent. And I wish I knew why the author chose this view. Rather, what he has chosen is the view of 'Isa b. Abban." (*'Umdat al-Hawashi 'ala Usul al-Shashi:* pp. 278-279)

173. Muslim reports it on the authority of Zayd ibn Thabit, Abu Hurayra, and 'A'isha. But the version quoted above is the version of Abu Hurayra and 'A'isha. The version of Zayd is that he heard the Prophet say, "Wudu is from whatever fire touches."

174. See *Usūl al-Shāshī:* p. 276

175. A saa' is a dry measure estimated as being equal to 1.053 liters

in volume or 2.24 kilograms in weight. See W. Hinz, *Islamische Masse und Gewichte* (Leiden, 1970).

176. Shaykh Al-Gangohi says, "...were he to act in accord with the hadith in this form also, the door to reflective opinion (*ra'y*) would be closed from every regard. Allah—the most high—has ordered us to employ analogy for He says, "So, take a moral lesson, O you who have eyes!" (Hashr: 2) The situation is that the transmitter is unpopular for having legal knowledge, while transmitting by meaning was something widely known and widespread among them. Perhaps, the transmitter would convey the hadith by meaning according to his understanding but committed an error and did not comprehend the intent of Allah's messenger , since it is of grave seriousness for one to be fully acquainted with all that he intended. For, surely he was given the broadness of brevity in speech (*jawāmi' al-kalim*). And one can only become acquainted [with his intent] through knowledge and scholarly endeavor. So when the transmitter is not a *mujtahid*, he will not be fully acquainted with all that he meant soundly. How then can his words be relied upon and taken in relinquishment of legal analogy? So, because of this necessity, the hadith is abandoned and legal analogy is acted upon. But, this is not a slight of Abū Hurayra and a belittlement of him. Nay! God forbid! Rather, it is merely an elucidation of a minute scholarly observation at this point." ('*Umdat al-Hawashi:* 278)

177. See *Al-Wajiz fi Usul al-Fiqh* of Zaydan: 170-171, and '*Ilm Usul al-Fiqh of Khallaf*: 41.

178. This is also the view of Imam Malik.

179. Imam Ibn Taymiyya says, "And those who reported that Ahmed used to use the weak hadith which is neither *sahih* nor *hasan* as proof, such a person is considered to be in error. Rather, it was in the custom of Ahmed b. Hanbal and those scholars before him that the hadith was of two types: sahih and *da'if*. The *da'if* (weak) report according to them divided into one that is to be abandoned completely (matruk) that cannot be presented as proof, and to one that is of fair grading (hasan), just as the weakness experienced in a person due to illness divides into one that is life-threatening that bars one from donating from his estate and one that leads to a light weakness that does not bar one

from donating [his wealth]. The first to be known for dividing the hadith into three divisions—sahih, *hasan*, and *da'if*—is Abu 'Isa Al-Tirmidhi in his *Jami'*. The hasan report according to him is the one that has a number of chains of narration and does not possess a transmitter who has been accused of something incriminating and it does not contradict the versions of more reliable transmitters. This kind of hadith and its likes is what Ahmed refers to as *da'if* (weak) but is utilised as proof." (*Qa'ida Jalila fi al-Tawassul wa al-Wasila:* p. 71)

180. Here, it is important to point out that most Muslims of the Sunni tradition have adopted this view that only sahih hadiths may be utilised and have been taught that this is the opinion of all the Imams of the Salaf when in fact it is only the view of Shāfi'ī.

181. Tilmasani says, "As for reports of undisclosed intermediaries (*irsal*), it is for a non-Companion to relate a hadith about the Messenger of Allah without specifying the Companion he received it from." (*Miftah al-Wusul* p. 349)

182. Imam Al-Zurqānī says in his Sharh of the *Bayquniyya*, "And they differed about the authoritativeness of the *mursal* narration. Malik and Ahmed in the popular narrations about them, Abu Hanifa and his followers from the jurists, legal theorists, and hadith scholars all held the view that such reports are authoritative in the rulings of religious practice (*Ahkam*) and other matters." (*Al-Manzuma al- Bayquniyya bi Sharh Al-Zurqani ma'a Hashiya al-Shaykh Al-Ajhuri:* 144)

183. The view of Malik and the overwhelming majority of Malikis is that whenever the narrator is trustworthy his *mursal* report is acceptable. Tilmasānī says in his *Miftāh* in response to objections to *mursal* reports, "The response with our comrades is that the *mursal* reports are acceptable to us. The Successors (*Tabi'un*)—may Allah be pleased with them—were incessant in transmitting hadiths with undisclosed intermediaries and presenting them as proof due to the knowledge that they only report without such disclosure on the authority of trustworthy people." (*Miftāh al-Wusūl* pp. 354-355) Abū Hanīfa and most of his disciples, most of the Mu'tazila, one narration about Imam Ahmed, and a group of the scholars of hadith are of the view that *mursal* reports are accepted absolutely. In another narration

about Imam Ahmed, he did not accept them. Most scholars of hadith, some of the jurists (*fuqahā'*), and some legal theorists (*ahl al-usul*) are of the view that *mursal* reports are not accepted. (*Tahqiq Farkush 'ala Miftah al-Wusul* pp. 353-354)

184. Juwayni says of Shafi'i, "He—may Allah show him mercy—said, "The *mursal* reports of Ibn al-Musayyab are good (*hasana*)" [...] He said in *Kitab al-Risala:* "Whenever the righteous and trusted person conveys a *mursal* report and the people act in accord with his mursal report, I accept it." (*Al-Burhan fi Usul al-Fiqh:* 1/245)

185. Imam al-Juwaynī says about the matter of accepting and acting on the *mursal* hadiths, "Abu Hanifa is one who reports all of them, accepts them, [and] acts in accord with them. Shafi'i—may Allah be pleased with him—does not act in accord with any portion of them." (*Al-Burhān* 1/243)

186. Imam al-Juwayni says in his *Waraqat*, "Reports divide into those that are uncorroborated (*ahad*) and those that are indisputably authentic (*mutawatir*)...The uncorroborated are those that oblige action but do not oblige definitive knowledge due to the possibility of error occurring in their regard. They divide into two divisions: *mursal* and *musnad*. The *musnad* type is the one whose chain of transmission is connected. The *mursal* type is the one whose chain of transmission is not connected. If it happens to be one of the *mursal* narrations of one other than the Sahaba, it is not authoritative, unless it is one of the *mursal* narrations of Sa'id b. al-Musayyab. For verily they have been inspected and found to be connected in their chains (*masanid*)." (*Sharh al-Waraqat fi 'Ilm al-Uaul:* p. 12)

187. 'Abd Al-Karim Zaydan says, "The madhhab of Shafi'i is to accept [the *mursal* reports] with conditions. Among them are: [1] that it be one of the *mursal* reports of one of the senior Successors, like Sa'id b. al-Musayyab; [2] that it be related with a connected chain from a different path, or it conforms with the statement of a Companion, or if most scholars pass fatwa in accord with it." (*Al-Wajiz:* 173) So according to this inclusion, Shafi'i accepts the mursal hadith without consideration of its chain being connected in certain instances. And Allah knows best.

188. Suyuti says, "Ibn Salah and the author (Nawwawi) did not men-

tion here as in the remainder of their works anything more than this condition i.e. for the hadith to relate to the topic of meritorious works and the like. However, Shaykh al-Islām (Ibn Hajar) stated three conditions for it: [1] that the weakness not be severe, such that the lonesome reports of liars, those accused of lying, and those who are known for committing serious errors are excluded from consideration. Al-'Ala'i conveyed agreement on this point; [2] that it (the hadith) fall under a [religious] foundation that is acted upon; and [3] that one not believe when acting upon it that it is something confirmed. Rather, one is to believe with caution." He (Ibn Hajar) also said: "These two [conditions] were mentioned by Ibn 'Abd Al-Salam and Ibn Daqiq al-'Id. It has been said: "It is absolutely impermissible to act upon them (i.e. weak hadiths)." Abu Bakr b. Al-'Arabi said it. It has also been said: "They may be acted upon absolutely." And the ascription of that view to Abu Dawud and Ahmed has already been mentioned and that they held that to be stronger than the opinion of men." (*Tadrib*: 196-197)

189. p. 3

190. *Qa'ida Jalila:* 71

191. This can be found in Suyuti's *Tadrib al-Rawi:* p. 196. He also says in his commentary, "Of those this view has been reported about are: Ibn Hanbal, Ibn Mahdi, and Ibn al-Mubarak. They said: "When we report regarding the lawful and unlawful, we are strict. But when we report regarding the meritorious acts and the like, we abandon strictness.""

192. This is based on the well-known narration that the Prophet said, "Whenever the judge endeavors and hits the mark, he has two rewards. But when he endeavors and misses the mark, he has [only] one reward" (Bukhari, Ibn Majah, Nasa'i, and Ahmed). Notice that the Prophet restricted this reward in both cases to the learned, not the unlearned.

193. *Tirmidhi*: hadith #2952. Ibn Taymiyya also reports it in his *Muqaddima fi Usul al-Tafsir:* 51 along with variant narrations of the hadith.

194. Abu Dawud reports it in *Tahara*: Chapter 125 and grades it as *hasan*.

Biography

- Abadi, 'Abd al-Rahman Sharaf b. Amir al-'Azim. *'Awn al-Ma'bud 'ala Sunan Abi Dawud*. Amman: Bayt al-Afkar al-Dawliyya
- Al-'Arabi, Qadi Abu Bakr Muhammad b. 'Abd Allah. *Ahkam Al-Quran*. Mecca: Maktaba Dar al-Bazz, 1416/1996
- Al-Bayquni, 'Umar b. Muhammad b. Fatuh. *Al-Manzuma al-Bayquniyya bi Sharh Al-Zurqani ma'a Hashiya al-Shaykh Al-Ajhuri*. Beirut: Dar al-Kutub al-'Ilmiyya, 1420/1999
- Al-Gangohi, Muhammad Fayd al-Hasan. *'Umdat al-Hawashi 'ala Usul al-Shashi*. Beirut: Dar al-Kitab al-'Arabi, 1402/1982
- Ibn Taymiyya, Ahmed. *Qā'ida Jalila fi al-Tawassul wa al-Wasila*. Beirut: Dar al-Kutub al-'Ilmiyya, 1418/1998
- *Muqaddima fī Usul al-Tafsir*. Cairo: al-Matba'at al-Salafiyya wa Maktabatuha, 2nd Ed. 1385 AH
- Al-Ghazali Abu Hamid Muhammad. *Al-Mustasfa' min Usul al-Fiqh*. Beirut: Dar al-Arqam b. Abi al-Arqam, 1414/1994
- Al-Juwayni, Abu al-Ma'ali Imam al-Haramayn. *Al-Burhan fi Usul al-Fiqh*. Beirut: Dar al-Kutub al-'Ilmiyya, 1418/1997
- Al-Mahalli, Muhammad b. Ahmed. *Sharh al-Waraqāt fī 'Ilm Usul al-Fiqh*. Beirut: Dar al-Fikr.
- Al-Nawwawi, Yahya b. Sharaf. *Sahih Muslim bi Sharh al-Imam Abu Zakariyya al-Nawwawi*. Beirut: Dar al-Fikr, 1415/1995
- Al-Siddiq, Ahmed b. Muhammad. *Masālik al-Dilālat Fi SharhMasā'il al-Risāla*. Casablanca: Dar al- Rashad al-haditha,

1423/2002

- Al-Suyuti, 'Abd al-Rahman. *Tadrīb al-Rawi fi Sharh Taqrib al-Nawawi.* Beirut: Dar al-Fikr, 1414/1993
- Al-Tanukhi, Sahnun b. Sa'id. *Al-Mudawwana Al-Kubrā.* Beirut: Dar al-Fikr, 1419/1998
- Al-Tilmasani, Muhammad b. Ahmed. *Miftah al-Wuuul ilā Bina' al-Furu' 'ala al-Usul.* Beirut: Mu'assasat al-Rayyan, 1419/1998
- Al-Tirmidhi, Abu 'Isa Muhammad b. 'Isa. *Jāmi' al-Tirmidhi.* Riyadh: Dar al-Salam, 1420/1999
- Zaydan, 'Abd al-Karim. *Al-Wajiz fi Usul al-Fiqh.* Beirut: Mu'assasat al-Risala, 1425/2004
- Al-Zurqani, Muhammad b. 'Abd al-Baqi. *Sharh al-Zurqani 'ala Muwatta al-Imam Malik.* Beirut: Dar al-Kutub al-'Ilmiyya